WHAT IS

RATIONAL EMOTIVE

BEHAVIOUR THERAPY?

A PERSONAL AND PRACTICAL GUIDE
SECOND EDITION

Ann MacInnes

BY

WINDY DRYDEN, JACK GORDON

& MICHAEL NEENAN

Published by GALE CENTRE PUBLICATIONS, LOUGHTON, ESSEX, IG10 1SQ

Published by Gale Centre Publications
Loughton, Essex
IG10 1SQ

© Windy Dryden & Jack Gordon, 1990.
Second Edition Windy Dryden, Jack Gordon & Michael Neenan, 1997.

Printed in Great Britain by Metloc Printers Ltd., Loughton, Essex

British Library Cataloguing in Publication Data

A CIP record for this book is available from the British Library

ISBN 1 870258 08 8

CONTENTS

PREFACE

Why a personal and practical guide?

The personal and practical guides aim to help you understand what a particular therapy is about and what it feels like to experience it and to be a therapist in it. The check lists, descriptions, exercises and case histories in the guides are designed to allow you to form an individual study programme or a study programme with a group of colleagues. This programme will not turn you into therapists nor will it enable you to work on a deep level on therapeutic problems and it is not designed with either of these aims in mind. What it will do is give you an experience of how the therapeutic method works by suggesting practical exercises you can do yourself. It will also give you an experience of what it feels like to be a therapist giving that sort of therapy, the sort of problems for which the therapy can be used to help and the likely outcome.

After this study programme you will at the very least know what the therapy is about and be able to talk coherently about it. You will also have a better idea of whether you would want to be a client in that form of therapy and whether you would want to develop an expertise in it. I also hope that experienced and practising therapists will be able to find elements in the therapies described which they will be able to use to supplement and develop their own skills.

It is generally a requirement of training as a therapist that the therapist undertake therapy. It often strikes me as odd that therapists writing about their work make only scant references to their own therapy.

Therapists seem to be particularly reticent in talking about their own therapy, yet at the same time maintain that there is no stigma attached to therapy.

Therapy is not a science, it is an art and research has shown that the individual qualities of the therapist are often more significant than the method used. It seems odd that so little writing about therapy includes the personal experiences of therapists and their difficulties and failures in therapy.

PREFACE TO THE SECOND EDITION
The 'What Is' Series Ten Years On

Little did I think when I published the first edition of What Is Psychotherapy in 1987 that ten years later this 28 page self produced booklet would have developed into a fully fledged series of books with best-selling authors like Windy Dryden, Phillip Burnard, Tony Merry and Eric Whitton, with myself as the series editor.

1997 brings with it the second edition of What is Rational Emotive Therapy, now called What is Rational Emotive Behaviour Therapy, and What is Transactional Analysis. What is REBT has been completely reworked to take account of new directions in this powerful form of self help therapy. What is TA has new sections and has been general updated. Both books have new covers.

The change in the covers seems to reflect the way the series has changed. To begin with the cover designs were done by a friend, Lizzie Spring and they reflected something of our personal understanding of the subject matter of the books. While I will remain ever grateful to Lizzie for her help and support her designs were not "commercial book covers" and the distributors wanted commercial covers. Did I say distributors? When I started out I published and distributed the books myself but now they and other Gale Centre Publications titles are distributed by Airlift which is one of the biggest distributors of psychology and self help books in the country. So we have certainly grown up in ten years.

But you can't judge a book by its cover and as an editor it has been warming to hear and read so many positive remarks made by readers of these books and as stock sells out it is most rewarding to see new editions coming out which have been fully revised and updated. Of course all authors like to see their work in print, but I like to think they have a special place in their hearts for their own particular "What is ..." because the format has relieved them of the demands of a more commercial publisher and allowed them to write something really personal. As psychotherapy is developing, the personal, is becoming more and more distanced from the demands for professionalisation and while I welcome a more professional and therefore reliable profession, I hope that there will always be a place for the personal and even slightly quirky.

Psychotherapy and Counselling have moved on since 1987. It was often referred to as the only growth industry during the recession. The Rugby Conference has developed into the UK Council for Psychotherapists with its Register of Psychotherapists published annually by Routledge. Now the British Association of Counselling is setting up a similar register. All of this means that Psychotherapy and Counselling are becoming more and more established and regulated. This is not to the taste of everybody but whether we like it of not it is the way of the future and recently the arts therapists (art, drama, music and movement therapists) have at last completed the parliamentary procedures which will lead to these therapists being able to refer to themselves as chartered. This will not only protect their title but also give them a boost to their status putting them on a part with other chartered practitioners.

As professionalisation continues, there is a danger of the client or patient being alienated. I notice in my own practice that preliminary enquiries centre on my qualifications and that people trust me because I am qualified. While in some ways this may be a good thing it often weakens the power of the client to decide, for themselves, if they are getting what they want and need. This means that being well informed in your own right is even more important, so that you are in a position to challenge the professionals if you think that they are not meeting your needs. I therefore expect this series to continue its future life as people continue to ask themselves exactly "What is ....?"

Derek Gale
Loughton, 1997

CHAPTER ONE

THE FINGER POINTING EXERCISE

When I (WD) run an introductory workshop on Rational Emotive Behaviour Therapy, I usually begin with an exercise that I call The Finger Pointing Exercise. I want you to imagine that you are attending the workshop as a participant and to monitor your reactions as I take you through the exercise.

"Think of a secret that you would not want anyone else to know about, not even your best friend. It's a secret - something of which you are ashamed. Your secret could involve an action that you feel particularly ashamed about, or it could be a personal weakness that you would not want anyone else to know about. Now, continue to think about it, because in a moment I am going to walk among you and I am going to point a finger at one of you. When I do that, I want the person concerned to go to the centre of the room. Then I am going to ask that person to disclose the secret in front of the rest of the group."

At this point in the exercise I walk round the circle in front of everybody with my pointed finger raised above my head, poised to point at the person I will single out to disclose his or her secret in public. I walk in front of all the workshop participants several times around the circle. But, I do not point at anybody! Instead, I say, "OK, I'm now going to ask you to share your feelings. What did you actually feel as I walked round and round in front of you, my finger poised in the air and about to point directly at any one of you - perhaps even you?"

What would your feelings have been if you had been sitting in that circle of workshop participants? Keep your feelings in mind as I am now going on to discuss some common emotional reactions that workshop participants have said they experienced in response to this exercise.

SOME EMOTIONAL REACTIONS TO THE FINGER POINTING EXERCISE

Quite a few participants have said that they experienced anxiety. Let me give you a couple of examples. One participant, Jock, said that his anxiety was related to the negative reactions that he anticipated he would receive from the rest of the group in response to disclosing his secret. On further exploration, Jock's anxiety was related to the following:

He predicted that the others in the group would consider him a bad person for doing such a "shameful act" in the past, However, this prediction was only part of the story. Jock not only had a preference that other people in the group would think well of him, but he was also demanding that they must approve of him. From this "must" he then concluded, "Because other people absolutely must approve of me, and I predict that they won't, then

(a) It would be awful if they thought badly of me,

(b) I couldn't stand it if they thought badly of me, and

(c) I would be a bad person if they thought that I was a bad person."

Freda, another workshop participant, also reported feeling anxious during the exercise. However, her anxiety was related to a different aspect of the situation. Freda believed that, if she was chosen to reveal her secret, she would have no choice but to do just that. Freda's belief was not only based on her desire to act in a cooperative manner in the group, but, in addition, she believed that she absolutely had to act cooperatively, even though she did not want to. Freda drew the following conclusions from this demand:

(a) It would be terrible if she did not act in a cooperative manner,

(b) She could not tolerate being non-cooperative, and

(c) She would think less of herself if she did not cooperate by disclosing her secret.

Other participants reported feeling concerned, but not anxious. For example, Heather stated that she experienced concern during the exercise. Her feelings of concern stemmed from a preference, not a demand. Her preference was:

(a) I don't really want to behave in this way but there's no reason why I must not decline Dryden's invitation to disclose my secret.

(b) If I declined the invitation and other people in the group thought badly of me, that would be unfortunate, but not terrible.

(c) It's uncomfortable to be disapproved of, but I can stand it. It's hardly unbearable, and

(d) I can accept myself in spite of others' disapproval and not put myself down.

George also reported experiencing concern in this exercise. In this case George's concern was related to discomfort, and stemmed from his belief.

(a) I prefer to be comfortable in workshop situations, but there is no reason why I have to experience comfort. Discomfort is just that, uncomfortable but not awful, and

(b) I can put up with the discomfort and see what happens. There is no reason why I can't stand these feelings of discomfort.

Yet a further group of participants reported that they experienced anger in response to this exercise. Madeleine was one such participant. She considered that my behaviour was unbecoming of a workshop participant in that I was unfairly putting pressure on other people. However, her angry feelings did not stem from the presumed fact of my acting unfairly towards the group. Instead, Madeleine's anger was created by her demands, namely that

(a) I, as a workshop leader, must not act unfairly,

(b) It's scandalous and terrible that I do so,

(c) She cannot tolerate my behaviour, and

(d) I am something of a rotten person for acting in this manner.

In fact, this anger related to my "unfair behaviour" is a fairly common reaction among workshop participants.

However, other people reported feeling annoyed at my behaviour, rather than angry at me. Susan, for example, also considered that I was acting unfairly, but she did not demand that I must not do so. Her belief was related to a non-demanding desire. She reported her beliefs in this way:

(a) I strongly prefer Professor Dryden not to act in this way but there is absolutely no reason why he must not do so.

(b) It's too bad that he acts in this unfair manner, but it isn't terrible, and

(c) He's a fallible human being for acting in what I consider to be a wrong manner, but he is not condemnable for it.

A minority of workshop participants reported positive feelings in response to this exercise. For example, Harriet's feelings were based on the hope that I would choose her to report on her secret in front of the group, because if I did that, it would give her the opportunity to practice her newly developed assertive skills. She was actually looking forward to saying, "No! I refuse to tell you my secret." Her feelings changed to disappointment when I didn't choose her, or indeed anybody.

Michael reported having feelings of pleasure in response to this exercise. He focused on the fact that he was learning a good technique that he could use with his own students and that he was getting what he wanted from the workshop: new ideas.

Now, how did you feel? We'll come back to your reactions at the end of our discussion of this exercise.

THE PURPOSE OF THE FINGER POINTING EXERCISE

My aim in carrying out the Finger Pointing Exercise is to teach workshop participants that it is not the objective situation that people are in that makes them experience feelings. The emotional reactions that people experience in relation to events in their lives are created and maintained by both the inferences they make about these events, and particularly, their beliefs and evaluations about these inferences. Notice how some of the workshop participants focused on "threatening" aspects of the situation. This was particularly true of those who experienced anxiety and concern. But, also note that these inferences on their own did not discriminate between those who experienced anxiety and those who experienced concern. While inferences that threat exists in a given situation limit people to experiencing anxiety or concern, the inference on its own does not account for the experience of either anxiety or concern. The deciding factor here is the evaluation that people make of their inferences. Thus, those who experienced anxiety not only inferred that the given situation was threatening, they also evaluated it as "terrible", as a situation that must not exist and which they could not stand if it were to come about. Moreover, some of those experiencing anxiety would devalue themselves in certain circumstances were the threat to materialise.

It is important to note that those who experienced concern, rather than anxiety during the exercise, also focused on the possibility of threat arising from the exercise, but these people evaluated the threat in more flexible ways. In other words, they did not like the idea that the situation might be threatening, and they definitely preferred that a threatening situation would not arise. but - and this is the crucial point - they did not demand that a threatening situation absolutely must not exist.

Now, compare these reactions above with the feelings of anger which some participants reported they experienced during the Finger Pointing Exercise. Those people who felt angry tended to make inferences about my behaviour, namely, that I was acting in an unfair manner. This inference influenced them to experience either anger or annoyance, but as in the preceding example of anxiety or concern, this inference on its own was not the deciding factor in determining which emotional reaction would predominate. Once again, it was these participants' belief or evaluation that was linked to the inference that decided the emotional outcome. Thus, participants who demanded that I must not act unfairly tended to experience anger, while those other participants who merely preferred that I did not act unfairly, but refrained from changing their preference to a demand that I must not act unfairly, tended to experience annoyance or displeasure.

Of those other workshop participants who experienced positive feelings of pleasure, note that their feelings were linked to inferences that centred on the fulfilment of some desire. These participants were getting what they wanted; the exercise was, in some way, fulfilling their desires of what they wanted to get out of the workshop.

Now, what were your experiences while you attended in your imagination as a participant in this workshop exercise? Did you experience anxiety? Or was it merely concern? What, if any, threatening inference were you placing on the reality of my walking around with my finger pointed in the air, ready to single someone out to expose a personal secret in front of the group? If anxiety was your predominant feeling, look for the demands you were making in your head about this threat. Look, until you find, exaggerated evaluations such as, "It's awful, I can't stand it!" Were you devaluing yourself in your mind if the aspects you found personally threatening in the situation were to come true?

If concern, not anxiety, was your predominating feeling, identify your non-dogmatic preferences about the threat occurring. They will be found to be of the order: " I don't want the threat to occur, but there is no reason why it must not happen". Then look for your evaluation such as: "It's unfortunate if what I fear actually comes about, but it isn't terrible. "Terrible" is a figment of my imagination. If others in the group disapprove of me and consider me weak for feeling afraid and showing concern, that is unfortunate, but I can still accept myself in the face of their criticism."

Did you experience feelings of anger or annoyance? Once again look for the inferences you made concerning my behaviour. Did you regard it as unfair? Was I transgressing some rule or standard that you held concerning appropriate leader behaviour in workshop situations? If you felt angry, what demands were you making in your head about me? For example, were you demanding that I must not act in the manner that I was acting? Were you telling yourself that it was terrible that I was acting in this manner? Did you believe that you couldn't tolerate this deplorable situation? And what sentences were you turning over in your mind to devalue me on account of my "terrible" behaviour?

If you felt annoyed or displeased rather than angry or enraged, look for the beliefs that stemmed from your preferences rather than from your musts. Were you, for example, wishing or preferring that I would act differently but not demanding that I absolutely must act differently? Did you convince yourself that it may have been bad that I was acting in this way, but that it was hardly terrible or awful, and that you could tolerate the situation and accept me as a person who was making an error without in any way, putting me down as a human for making an error?

If you experienced positive feelings, which of your desires were being met during your imagined participation in the exercise? You may be interested to know that whenever I have carried out this exercise I have never actually asked anybody to come out into the centre of the group and disclose their "secret" to the other workshop participants. I also tell the group that this is the only time during the workshop that I will intentionally act in a manner designed to conceal my true purpose. Remember that my purpose is to show the group that people have emotional reactions to their inferences and their beliefs about situations, and not to the situations themselves. Inferences influence people in the kind of emotional reactions they are likely to experience, but they do not of themselves determine which particular emotion they will experience.

Rather, it is the evaluative beliefs that people hold about events and their inferences of events that are the most important determinant of the way people feel.

CHAPTER TWO

THREE MORE EXPERIENTIAL EXERCISES

IDENTIFYING FEELINGS OF HURT AND DISAPPOINTMENT

In this exercise we want you to imagine a time when you felt very hurt about something that someone close to you had done. Vividly imagine the behaviour of the other person and really get in touch with your feelings of hurt. Now, see if you can identify the beliefs that you had at the time that underpinned your feelings of hurt. In particular, look for the demands that you were making about the other person. For example, were you demanding that the other person must not behave in the way that he or she did, particularly if the other person was a loved one or family member who ideally should not have treated you in the manner that they did? Were you demanding that because you didn't deserve to be treated in this way, therefore the other person absolutely must not treat you in this way?

Let's assume you have identified those demands with which you eventually made yourself feel hurt. You start off with making demands. Now, what conclusions follow these demands? The conclusions, the evaluations you relate to your demands are the determinants of your hurt. What kind of evaluations? Well, were you, for example, telling yourself that it's terrible or horrible that the other person acted in this betraying manner towards you? Were you telling yourself that you can't stand the other person's behaviour and that he or she was a rotten person for behaving in the way they did? Perhaps you were feeling sorry for yourself. "Poor me! What a rotten world this is for allowing such behaviour to go on!" Here, you will note that feelings of self-pity are often present when you feel hurt. Honestly look for these feelings and acknowledge that they exist when they are present. Ask yourself whether you were in any way putting yourself down. For example, were you convincing yourself that because the other person had treated you badly in a way you previously thought you didn't deserve, perhaps they were right after all and that you really were an undeserving, worthless person?

In the original Finger Pointing Exercise, you will recall that I (WD) made the point that in REBT we distinguish between two types of negative emotions (e.g. anxiety versus concern, anger versus annoyance). As will be discussed later, feelings like anger and anxiety are regarded in REBT as unhealthy negative emotions in that they tend to lead to self-defeating and other unwanted consequences, whereas feelings of concern and annoyance are seen as healthy negative emotions because they help the individual to adjust and to cope more effectively with negative life events. Feelings of hurt are regarded in REBT as unhealthy negative emotions because they also frequently lead to self-defeating outcomes as well as doing little to improve personal relationships. It is a common experience that people who feel hurt often withdraw from the other person in a kind of sulking hostility. The constructive alternative to "hurt" is "disappointment". Now, try this exercise in disappointment.

Close your eyes and vividly imagine another time in your life when another person whom you were close to, treated you badly or inconsiderately and unfairly. Or you could have been betrayed as described in the exercise on hurt. This time, however, choose an example where you felt disappointed, rather than hurt, about the experience. Try to choose an example that was as serious as the example you chose when doing the exercise on hurt, but one to which you responded with disappointment rather than with hurt. Close your eyes and vividly imagine that circumstance. See the person acting in the way that they did, and relive those feelings of disappointment you experienced at the time. Right, now let's see if we can distinguish between the beliefs that underpin hurt and the beliefs that underpin disappointment.

While you are re-living your feelings of disappointment, look for your non-dogmatic beliefs. These will take the form of desires, even strong desires or preferences that the other person had acted differently, but however desirable that might have been, there was no reason why they absolutely had to have acted any differently from the way they indubitably did act. If you found traces of demandingness, for example, demands that the other person must not have treated you in the way they did treat you, the chances are you are experiencing hurt, rather than disappointment. In that case, search your mind again for an example where your response was strong disappointment, and once you have found it, actively look for your non-demanding preferences.

Next, look for the conclusions that you came to following your non-demanding preference(s). Typically, these will be evaluative statements such as:

(a) "It's unfortunate that the other person acted in this way, but it's not terrible or awful. I can definitely stand it although I'll never like it.

(b) Just because the other person is acting in such a bad manner, that doesn't mean that he or she is a good-for-nothing, or that the world is a rotten place for allowing such things to happen. I'm not a poor unfortunate soul who is being treated in a terrible manner, but simply a person who is not being treated as I think I deserve to be, or would like to be treated. Tough! There's no reason why I have to get what I think I deserve.

(c) I can still accept myself in the face of the other person's poor behaviour. Just because the other person is acting badly towards me that doesn't mean anything about me as a person in my own eyes.

(d) I can openly discuss with the other person the reasons for their poor behaviour while still accepting myself and in no way downing myself for being treated unfairly or inconsiderately."

How did you fare in these two exercises? If you've been successful you will see that in both feelings of hurt and disappointment, there are similar inferences involved. These inferences are that some other person has acted towards you in an unfair or betraying manner. However, what gives the experience of hurt on the one hand, and disappointment on the other hand their distinctive character, are the different beliefs involved. We have suggested that hurt is based upon a demanding attitude, that the other person must not act in the way they did, whereas in disappointment the belief is a more flexible one; in disappointment, you prefer, you wish that the other person did not act in such a bad manner, but you do not demand that they must act differently from the way that they did act.

In addition, the conclusions you draw from these beliefs are different. In hurt, there are the conclusions that "it's terrible, I can't stand it, and the world is no good for allowing such conditions to exist." Also, you are probably telling yourself that you are diminished, or less worthy as a person as a result of such treatment being meted out to you.

By contrast, when you experience disappointment, and refrain from changing your feelings to those of hurt, your conclusions are of the form:

(a) It is unfortunate, but hardly terrible that I am being treated in this way, but I can stand what I don't like and the world is hardly a rotten place just because such unfortunate behaviour takes place.

(b) I'm certainly not a person to be pitied, either by myself or others, nor will I put myself down in response to the other person's poor behaviour towards me.

IDENTIFYING FEELINGS OF GUILT AND REMORSE

This exercise is similar to the one above, but here you will be asked to identify an occasion when you felt guilty and a time when you felt remorseful about breaking your own moral code. Before we begin the exercise we want to make the following point about the word "guilt". In REBT, guilt is commonly used to mean feelings of guilt as distinct from guilty acts. You may be guilty of committing some misdeed, for example, but your feelings about the act are not the same thing as the act itself. Feelings of guilt are regarded as self-defeating and unhelpful or even harmful for reasons which will become obvious later.

First, remember a time when you felt very, very guilty about breaking your own moral code. The transgression of your code may have been related to something that you did (an act of commission), or something that you failed to do (an act of omission). Vividly picture in your mind your violation of your own moral code and stick with the feelings of guilt even though they are likely to be quite painful.

Now, while still remaining with your feelings of guilt see if you can identify the beliefs that underpin those feelings. For example, look for the demands that you made upon yourself. Were you telling yourself not only do I prefer to adhere to my moral code, but I absolutely must not break it under any circumstances? If you find such a belief, look for the conclusions you drew from this belief. Search for statements such as:

(a) "It's awful that I broke my moral code,

(b) I can't stand my behaving like that, and

(c) I'm a damnable, rotten person for doing so and less worthy in my own eyes than if I hadn't acted in this immoral manner."

Now, let's move on to the second step of this exercise, which is identifying feelings of remorse. This time, think of an occasion when you once again broke your moral code and try to make it as serious a breach as the one you identified in the first part of this exercise on guilt. This time, however, choose a violation to which you responded with remorse, rather than guilt. Vividly imagine yourself breaking your moral code and really get in touch with your feelings of remorse. Once you have done this, look for the rational beliefs that underlay your feelings of remorse. Look for statements like:

(a) "I really dislike breaking my moral code, but there's no reason why I absolutely must not break it.

(b) It's very unfortunate that I broke my moral code on this occasion, but it isn't terrible.

(c) This situation is bearable even though I admit it is most unfortunate, and

(d) I can accept myself as a fallible human being who did the wrong thing, and maybe I can learn something from my failure and possibly make amends, but I am not a rotten or less worthy person for having acted in such a bad way."

By now, you may see that while guilt and remorse share the same inference of events, that is, that the person concerned has broken his or her moral code, the two feelings can be discriminated by differences in the kind of evaluative beliefs that the person makes about such an inference. In guilt, the evaluations are absolutistic and dogmatic, in remorse they are more flexible and relative, more reality based.

EXERCISE ON PROCRASTINATION AND TAKING EFFECTIVE ACTION

In this exercise we want to help you to distinguish between the beliefs that underpin procrastination and those that underpin taking effective action. First, procrastination. While there are different kinds of procrastination, we want you to select an example where you put off doing something that was tedious but would have benefited you in the long run had you tackled the task at the time it arose. Let's assume that putting off this task was really self-defeating. But don't choose an example where you procrastinated because you were scared that if you did the task poorly you would condemn yourself for it. Take an example where the task was tedious, but not threatening to your sense of self. Close your eyes and vividly imagine you are faced with the choice of doing, or not doing, this particular task. See yourself procrastinating. Stay with that scene for a couple of minutes.

Let's see, now, if you can identify the implicit beliefs that drove you to procrastination. First of all, how would you have felt initially if you had done the tedious task? It is likely that your predictions about your feelings would have centred on experiences of discomfort. OK, now look for the demands that you made about these feelings of discomfort. When you find them, you will probably identify beliefs such as:

(a) "I must not be uncomfortable. It's terrible to do something that I really don't want to do, or feel like doing.

(b) I can't stand personal discomfort, and

(c) The world is a rotten, unfair place for giving me more discomfort than I should have. I don't deserve to have a difficult life."

Now, once again, think of a time similar to the first when you were faced with a tedious task that you knew would pay you to tackle promptly, rather than be put off to a time when you might feel more like tackling it. Make this example a time when you actually did the task promptly, and that the consequences of not doing it would have been the same as in the previous example you chose. Now, close your eyes and vividly picture yourself doing the tedious task. How did you get yourself to do it? Once again, in REBT we hold that the distinction lies in the type of beliefs that underpins these two different kinds of actions. If you look for these beliefs you will find statements of desire or preference, along the lines of:

(a) "I don't want to do this task, it's a real pain in the neck, but there's no reason why I must not do it now, and it would be better for me in the long term if I do buckle down and get cracking on it now; so I will.

(b) While it's too bad that this task is tedious, it's not terrible and I can definitely stand doing what I don't like. Tough!

(c) The world is neither good nor bad because I'm faced with tedious tasks, it just is the way it is."

In both these situations, the person is faced with a tedious task, and in each of them there are equally serious negative consequences for procrastinating behaviour. However, the distinction lies once again in the type of belief the person holds about the situation. Bear in mind that in procrastination the person doesn't experience immediate discomfort for putting off the disagreeable task. The procrastination protects you from the "pain" of doing the task there and then, but it generally makes things more difficult for you later, and most of the time you know that. Nevertheless, the beliefs you have about discomfort are implicit in accounting for your behaviour.

CHAPTER THREE

BASIC THEORETICAL IDEAS

Rational Emotive Behaviour Therapy is a theory of personality and a method of psychotherapy originated and developed by Albert Ellis, a clinical psychologist, in the 1950's. Ellis originally worked as a psychoanalyst, but became dissatisfied with psychoanalysis because it was, in his words, "inefficient", time-consuming and it did not produce very effective results. After experimenting with briefer forms of psychoanalytic forms of psychotherapy, Ellis was influenced by his longstanding interest in philosophy, particularly proponents of the Stoic school, of whom Epictetus is a good example. Epictetus stated that "men are disturbed, not by things, but by their views of things." Through his famous Meditations, the Roman emperor, Marcus Aurelius, publicized Stoic philosophy, and later philosophers such as Spinoza and Bertrand Russell helped to bring these views to the attention of the western world. It has been said that there is nothing new under the sun. This is partly true, in that everything has evolved from, or been constructed from, some antecedent or combination of antecedents. What was new about REBT was the coherent development of a philosophy and a set of psychological constructs into a workable and effective form of psychotherapy.

To emphasise the cognitive aspects of his therapy, and the methods of logical disputation derived from them, Ellis termed his new therapy "Rational Therapy". In 1961, this was changed to "Rational-Emotive Therapy", a name which stressed that the therapy did not neglect emotions. Finally, in 1993, Ellis changed the name of the approach to "Rational Emotive Behaviour Therapy", to emphasize that it did not neglect the behavioural dimension of human functioning. The name "Rational Emotive Behaviour Therapy" (or REBT) is a more accurate description of the therapy because REBT emphasises that cognition (or thinking), feeling and behaviour are inter-related and interacting processes which all have to be taken into account if treatment methods are to be effective. This point was stressed in Ellis's first major book on REBT, entitled Reason and Emotion in Psychotherapy (Ellis, 1962).

GOALS, PURPOSES AND RATIONALITY

According to REBT theory humans are happiest when we set up important life goals and purposes and actively strive to achieve these. In doing so, we had better acknowledge that we live in a social world and we are thus encouraged to develop a philosophy of enlightened self-interest, which means pursuing our own valued goals while demonstrating what Alfred Adler called social interest - a commitment to helping others achieve their valued goals and a commitment to making the world a socially and environmentally better place in which to live. Given that we will tend to be goal directed, rational in REBT theory means "that which helps people to achieve their basic goals and purposes whereas irrational means that which prevents them from achieving these goals and purposes" (Dryden, 1984, page 238). While rationality is not defined in any absolute sense, it does have four major criteria, (a) pragmatic, (b) logical, (c) reality based and (d) flexible. Thus, a more extended definition of rationality would be that which helps us to achieve our basic goals and purposes, that which is logical, that which is empirically consistent with reality and that which is non absolutist. Conversely, irrationality means that which prevents us from achieving our basic goals and purposes, that which is illogical, that which is empirically inconsistent with reality and that which is absolutist, dogmatic and musturbatory.

RESPONSIBLE LONG-RANGE HEDONISM

Rational Emotive Behaviour Therapy argues that humans are basically hedonistic in the sense that we seek to stay alive and to achieve a reasonable degree of happiness. Most people, also, wish to relate intimately with a few selected individuals of the same and/or the other sex. Rather than pointing to "pleasures of the flesh", hedonism in REBT involves the concept of personal meaning. A person may be said to be acting hedonistically when she is happy acting in a manner which is personally meaningful for her. The concept of responsible hedonism means that we are advised to again be mindful of the fact that we live in a social world, and that ideally, our personally meaningful activities should not gratuitously harm other individuals or the world we share, but, if possible, help to make that shared world a better place to live in for ourselves and for others.

REBT makes an important distinction between short-range and long-range hedonism and maintains that we are likely to be at our happiest when we achieve both our short-term and our long-term goals. However, we frequently defeat our best interests by going for short-term satisfaction even when we acknowledge that doing so will sabotage our gaining more worthwhile objectives in the longer term. For example, some people will knowingly risk putting their health in jeopardy in later years for the sake of enjoying an excessive consumption of some pleasant tasting but potentially harmful beverage. Many people strive to avoid discomfort in the present or immediate future even when it would be highly advisable to put up with the threatened discomfort in order to avoid an even greater and more prolonged discomfort later. A surgical operation may be put off because of the immediate discomfort it would entail; but if the outcome is an even more serious operation made necessary later on because of a worsening health condition, the consequence is a higher degree of pain and discomfort than if the lesser discomfort had been faced in the first place. In many similar ways, we sabotage our own best interests and block the realisation of our goals through our insistence on being comfortable, or at least, avoiding pain in the here and now. REBT therapists encourage their clients to achieve a thought-out, realistic balance between the pursuit of their short-term and their long-term goals, while being mindful of the fact that what represents a healthy balance for one person, may be just the opposite for another person. Each person is best able to make that decision herself or himself once the counsellor has drawn up and explained the hedonic calculus or balance sheet.

ENLIGHTENED SELF-INTEREST

Enlightened self-interest means that we pursue our goals and strive primarily for our own happiness while being mindful that others have an equal right to strive for what they regard as significant in their lives. If we cynically disregard the rights of others to pursue their own paths to happiness, such antisocial conduct may well backfire with unfortunate results for everyone. We are advised to treat other people properly, with due concern for their rights, partly because we want to be, in our turn, treated properly by others and partly because we want to help create the kind of world it is safe and beneficial for us to live in. Morality, when it is rational, is not based on self-sacrificing, but on self-interested motives. REBT does not say that self-sacrifice is never justifiable. There can be circumstances where an individual may, for a time, legitimately put the interests of others, especially close loved ones, before his or her own interests, if the individual finds personal meaning and happiness in doing so. However, when putting the interests of others first becomes overwhelming and apparently without some end in sight, REBT would hold that such self-sacrificing conduct is probably irrational in that it may not only be self-defeating, but may also subtly harm the person receiving such attention. Clearly, enlightened self-interest includes social interest. We live in a social world and would do well to remember that human happiness is maximised under favourable social and environmental conditions.

PHILOSOPHIC AND SCIENTIFIC EMPHASIS

REBT theory agrees with the ideas of George Kelly (1955) that we are scientists and are able to appreciate that our philosophies are basically hypotheses about ourselves, other people and the world around us, which need to be tested. This is best accomplished in conjunction with our philosophical abilities, particularly our ability to think critically about the logical and illogical aspects of our thought. However, REBT theory stresses that we are born philosophers as well as scientists. We have the ability to think about our thinking and to realise that we are highly influenced by our own implicit philosophies of life. These philosophies tend to be either relatively flexible and undogmatic, or musturbatory and absolutist. Ellis maintains that while we have a strong tendency, partly biologically based, to think and act irrationally, we also have the ability to think critically about our own thinking and to judge whether or not our hypotheses are consistent with perceived reality.

HUMANISTIC OUTLOOK

REBT is not only philosophical and scientific in orientation, but it takes a specific humanistic-existential approach to human problems and their solution. This view conceptualises humans as holistic and indivisible, goal-directed organisms who have importance in the world just because we are human and alive, and who have the right to continue to exist and to enjoy and fulfil ourselves. It emphasises the ability of humans to create and direct our own destinies, and it encourages humans to unconditionally accept ourselves with our limitations while at the same time encouraging us to work towards minimising our limitations. REBT agrees with the position of ethical humanism which "encourages people to live by rules emphasising human interests over the interests of inanimate nature, of lower animals or of any assumed natural order of deity" (Ellis, 1980, page 327). However, this does not mean being ecologically or environmentally insensitive, or advocating the mindless slaughter of animals. And while we may disagree with others' religious views, we nevertheless uphold their right to hold their religious views. This outlook acknowledges people as human and in no way as superhuman or subhuman.

TWO BASIC BIOLOGICAL-BASED TENDENCIES

REBT theory hypothesises that we have a biologically-based tendency to think irrationally and a similar tendency to think rationally. It thus differs from other approaches to therapy in emphasising the power of these biologically-based tendencies over the power of environmental conditions to affect human happiness, although it by no means neglects the contribution of these environmental conditions to influence human emotion and behaviour. The view that irrational thinking is largely determined by biological factors, although always interacting with influential environmental conditions, rests on the seeming ease with which we think crookedly and the prevalence of such thinking even among those of us who have been rationally raised. Ellis has noted in this regard that "even if everybody had had the most rational upbringing, virtually all humans would often irrationally change their individual and social preferences into absolutistic demands on (a) themselves (b) other people and (c) the universe around them" (Ellis, 1984, page 20).[1]

REBT theory states, however, that we have a second biological tendency and that is to think rationally and to work towards changing our irrational thinking. Thus we have the ability to identify our irrational thinking, to realise why it is irrational and to change it to a more rational version and to continually work towards minimising, although certainly not eradicating, the impact of our tendency to think irrationally.

TWO MAJOR CATEGORIES OF HUMAN DISTURBANCE

Ellis has noted that human psychological problems may be loosely divided into two major categories, (a) ego disturbance and (b) discomfort disturbance. Ego disturbance relates to the demands that we make of ourselves and the consequent negative self-ratings that we make about ourselves when we fail to live up to our self-imposed demands. Furthermore, ego disturbance issues may underpin what at first glance may appear to be us making demands upon others or life conditions. For example, I may be angry at you because you are acting in a way which I perceive to be a threat to my "self-esteem". The fact that my anger is directed outwardly towards you seemingly serves to protect my own "shaky self-esteem". For a fuller discussion of this type of anger, the reader is referred to chapter ten.

Discomfort disturbance, on the other hand, is much more related to the issue of human comfort. While the person may make demands about self, others and life conditions, the main issue in discomfort disturbance relates to dogmatic commands that comfort and comfortable life conditions must exist. As will be shown later, the healthy alternative to ego disturbance rests on a fundamental attitude of unconditional self-acceptance. This implies that we fully accept ourselves as human and essentially unratable. The healthy alternative to discomfort disturbance rests on a philosophy of attaining a high level of frustration tolerance, or discomfort tolerance whereby we are prepared to tolerate frustration of discomfort, not for the sake of it, but as a way of overcoming obstacles to our long-term happiness. In other words, when unpleasant conditions are, for a time, unavoidable, it is better to put up with these uncomfortable conditions while preparing oneself to change them

---

[1] For a full discussion of Ellis's arguments concerning the biological basis of irrationality see Ellis (1976)

in some constructive manner later, rather than getting all hot and bothered about the situation and thereby giving oneself two problems to deal with instead of only one.

THE THREE MAJOR MUSTS

Ellis originally identified 12 irrational ideas which from clinical observation he considered to be at the root of most emotional disturbance (for a full discussion of these core irrational ideas, the reader is advised to consult Ellis, 1962). Most people appear to believe several unrealistic ideas with unhappy results in terms of their emotions and behaviours. All of them consist of some form of absolutism - of unqualified demands and needs, instead of preferences or desires. There are virtually innumerable expressed variations of these core irrational beliefs but they all amount to the same thing in terms of their meaning. In fact, these 12 or so supreme dictates that people impose on themselves can be "collapsed" down to three main dictates that cause immense difficulties. You've heard of the "Holy Trinity". Well ours is the unholy or "Irrational Trinity"!

The first dictate is:

(1) "Because it would be highly preferable if I were outstandingly competent and/or loved, I absolutely should and must be; it's awful when I am not, and I am therefore a worthless individual."

The second irrational and unprovable idea is:

(2) "Because it is highly desirable that others treat me considerately and fairly, they absolutely should and must, and they are rotten people who deserve to be utterly damned when they do not."

The third impossible dictate is:

3) "Because it is preferable that I experience pleasure rather than pain, the world absolutely should arrange this and life is horrible, and I can't bear it when the world doesn't."

These three core irrational ideas and their various corollaries and subheadings constitute the main factors in what we term neurosis or emotional/behavioural malfunctioning. And this implies that unless clients are shown how to recognise and uproot their irrational belief systems and replace them with sounder, reality-orientated philosophies, they are unlikely to surrender their self-defeating ways of relating to themselves and the world, and eventually to learn positive self-helping approaches to life.

In REBT we maintain that if one is an empiricist and invents no absolute necessities or imperatives, it is almost impossible to become emotionally disturbed. Of course, you may still feel sad, or annoyed when faced with the inevitable, unfortunate aspects of living in the world. And when life goes well for you, you may feel joyful, or even ecstatic, "over the moon" as they say. "Rational" in REBT does not mean unemotional. Rather, the more determined you are to be self-accepting, hedonistic and what Maslow termed self-actualising, by using your head and other faculties, the more emotional and in touch with your feelings you will tend to be.

THE 3 X 2 DISTURBANCE MATRIX

It is possible to take the three basic "musts" and the two fundamental categories of human emotional disturbance to form a 3 x 2 disturbance matrix (see Figure 1). The reader will recall that the three basic musts are, in their simplest form: I must; you must; life conditions must, and that the two fundamental categories of emotional disturbance are: Ego Disturbance and Discomfort Disturbance.

Figure 1: The 3 x 2 Disturbance Matrix

	Ego	Discomfort
I must	A	B
You must	C	D
Life must	E	F

(A) Ego Disturbance - Demands about Self

In this type of disturbance, it is quite clear that the person concerned is making demands upon herself and the main issue is her attitude towards herself. The major derivative from the "must" is some aspect of self-damnation, for example:

(a) "I must do well in my exams; I must obtain my degree, and if I don't, I'm no good."

Also, an equivalent demand is:
(b) "I must be loved and approved by certain people in my life, and if I'm not, that proves I'm no good."

(B) Discomfort Disturbance - Demands about Self

Here, the person makes demands about herself, but the real issue concerns her attitude towards discomfort. For example, "I must obtain my degree, because if I don't, I might have to settle for some kind of tedious manual job and my life conditions would be terrible and I couldn't stand that."

(C) Ego Disturbance - Demands about Others

In this example, the person is making demands about the way another person must, or must not act, but the real issue centres round her attitude towards herself. This often occurs when the person is angry about somebody and takes the form of a demand that the other person must not act in a certain way, because that way involves what the angry person perceives as a threat to her own self-esteem. For example, "You must treat me nicely because if you don't, that proves that you don't think much of me, and that means that I am no longer any good as a person."

(D) Discomfort Disturbance - Demands about Others

Here, the person is making demands upon others, but the real issue concerns the realm of discomfort. For example, "You must treat me nicely and look after me because I couldn't stand the hard life I'd be faced with if you do not."

(E) Ego Disturbance - Demands about Life Conditions

On the surface, the person is making demands about some aspects of life conditions, but the real issue concerns her real attitude towards herself. As an example, "Life conditions under which I live must be easy for me, because if they are not then that's just proof of my own worthlessness."

(F) Discomfort Disturbance - Demands about Life Conditions

In this kind of disturbance we are dealing with a more impersonal from of low frustration tolerance. This type of discomfort is frequently seen when people lose their temper with inanimate objects, or in situations requiring a fair amount of patience. For example, "My car absolutely must not break down when I'm just about to use it, because I could not stand the frustration if it did." Or, "When I join a queue for some service, I must be served quickly because I can't stand delays in getting what I want."

PSYCHOLOGICAL INTERACTIONISM

REBT theory states that a person's thoughts, emotions and actions cannot be treated separately from one another. Rather, they are best conceptualised as being overlapping or interacting psychological processes. This is the principle of psychological interactionism. So, for example, when I think about something, I also tend to have an emotional reaction towards it and also a tendency to act towards it in some way. Equally, if I have a feeling about some person then I am likely to have some thoughts about that person, and also again, a tendency to act in a relation to that person in a certain manner. Similarly, if I act in a certain manner towards some person or object, my action is based on the way I think and feel about that person or object.

REBT is the best known for the emphasis it places on cognition and for its cognitive restructuring components. While it is true that REBT does emphasise the power of cognition to influence human happiness and disturbance, it fully acknowledges the affective and behavioural aspects and maintains that these fundamental human psychological processes almost always interact, and often in complex ways. Similarly, in this approach to psychotherapy, while cognitive restructuring methods are very important, they are by no means the sole methods in the therapeutic armamentarium. Rational Emotive Behaviour Therapists frequently use emotive, evocative and behavioural methods to encourage clients to change their thinking and acquire a more rational outlook on themselves and the world. REBT therapists are seldom just interested in promoting symptom removal. Instead, the therapist aims to help the client to examine and change some of his or her most basic values, particularly those values which have caused the client trouble in the past, and are likely to make the client disturbance-prone in the future. For example, if a client has a serious fear of failing on his job, the REBT therapist would not merely help him or her to overcome that particular fear, and to be less afraid in future of failing vocationally. Instead, the client would be helped to give up all exaggerated fears of failing at anything and shown how to generally minimise their basic awfulising tendencies. It is a characteristic of REBT that the usual goal of therapy is not only to eliminate the client's presenting symptoms, but to rid the client of many other non-reported symptom-creating propensities.

In short, REBT strives for the most elegant solution possible to the problem of emotional disturbance and is seldom content with palliative solutions. In order to achieve an elegant solution to clients' emotional problems, Rational Emotive Behaviour Therapists need to employ not only cognitive techniques to dismantle their clients' magical, empirically unvalidatable thinking but also a whole variety of behaviour modifying techniques, including role-playing, assertion training, desensitisation, operant conditioning and a number of emotive techniques such as shame-attacking exercises and humour. These methods are not used indiscriminately but within the REBT theoretical framework.

THREE IMPORTANT REBT INSIGHTS

There are three important REBT insights in this framework which we will now outline.

Insight No 1.

Our self-defeating behaviour is related to antecedent and understandable causes. However, these antecedent events did not, by themselves, cause clients' problems, but rather clients' beliefs about the antecedent events or circumstances created these problems. As we teach our clients, "You feel as you think, and your feelings, your behaviour and your thinking are all inter-related. External events, such as being criticised or mistreated when you were young may have contributed to your emotional and subsequent behavioural reactions, but they did not cause your reactions. In the main, you create your own feelings by the way you think about and evaluate whatever you perceive is happening to you."

Insight No 2.

This is the understanding that regardless of how clients disturbed themselves in the past, they are now disturbed because they still believe the irrational ideas with which they created their disturbed feelings in the past and that they are still actively reindoctrinating themselves with these unsustainable beliefs, not because they were previously "conditioned" to hold these beliefs and now do so "automatically", but because they are continually reinforcing these ideas by their present self-defeating actions or inaction in addition to their unrealistic thinking. In other words, it is clients' currently active self-propagandization that maintains their disturbed emotions and behaviour and enables these to hold sway over their life in the present. Until clients clearly accept responsibility for the continuation of these irrational beliefs, they are likely to make only feeble attempts to dispel them.

Insight No 3

This is the clear realisation and unflinching acknowledgement by clients that since it is their own human tendency to think crookedly that created emotional problems in the past, and that since these problems have persisted because of continued self-indoctrination in the present, there is nothing for it except hard work and practice if these irrational beliefs are to be uprooted and to remain uprooted until they wither to the point where they cease to be a problem. That means that repeated rethinking and disputing of irrational beliefs, together with repeated actions designed to undo them, are necessary if these beliefs are to be extinguished or minimised.

We conclude this section by briefly summarising the main points of REBT personality theory:

(1) Human beings are born with a distinct proneness to create their own emotional disturbances, and furthermore, learn to exacerbate that proneness through social and cultural conditioning.

(2) Humans have the ability to clearly understand how they originally acquired and have continued to maintain their emotional and dysfunctional behaviour, and to train themselves to change or eliminate their self-defeating beliefs and habits.

3) Self-reconditioning requires self-discipline (which humans can acquire) plus hard work and practice at understanding, contradicting and acting against their irrational and magical belief systems.

BASIC CONCEPTS: A BRIEF REVIEW

The main propositions of REBT may be summarised:

(1) REBT hypothesises that humans have a biologically-based tendency to think irrationally as well as a similar tendency to think rationally. On the one hand, we have powerful predispositions to preserve our lives, to seek pleasure and avoid pain, to use language, to think (often in highly creative ways), to organise our world, to love, to note and learn from our mistakes, and to actualise our potential for life and growth by experimenting with new individual lifestyles and social structures. On the other hand, we also have potent propensities to be self-destructive, hating, instant gratification seekers or short-range hedonists, to shirk self-responsibility, to repeat our mistakes over and again, and to be dogmatic, grandiose, intolerant and superstitious.

(2) Our tendencies to think and behave in self-destructive or self-limiting ways are exacerbated by our culture in general, and by our family groups in particular. We are conditionable by social influences as well as by innate or biological tendencies. But we are at our most suggestible state when we are young, although we are gullible more or less throughout our lives. In short, we have distinct biosocial tendencies to act in one way or another, and in this respect each individual is unique.

(3) As noted above, we tend to perceive, think, feel and behave interactionally. it follows that to understand and eliminate self-defeating or disturbed conduct it is desirable to use a variety of cognitive, emotive and behaviour-modification methods within an overall conceptual framework. We call this framework the ABC model of human disturbance, and it is to this that we now turn our attention.

THE ABC MODEL

The ABC model of emotional disturbance is a quick and effective technique for conceptualising clients' emotional problems, and for helping them to identify and uproot the irrational components of their belief systems which are responsible for creating and sustaining their upsetting emotions and dysfunctional behaviours. Let's suppose that some obnoxious event happens to an individual at point A. We call this the activating event. Now, let's suppose that the individual (in this case male) feels emotionally upset at point C. Point C represents the consequences(s) that accompany or follow the activating event (A). Now, our individual convinces himself of two radically different things at point B, which stands for his belief systems. First, the individual convinces himself of a healthy rational belief, namely "I definitely don't like what has happened to me (at point A) and I wish it did not exist. But it has happened, there's no denying it and it doesn't have to be different. Tough!" If the individual stayed with that belief, how would he feel? He'd feel disappointed, sorrowful, irritated, or frustrated, rather than upset, disorganised or panicked. Why? Well, because realistically speaking, it is unfortunate that some unpleasant event has occurred and his healthy feeling of annoyance may well motivate him to go back to the activating event at A and try to change it. Or if he can't change it, he can perhaps try to take steps to avoid it happening again in future. So, he may rationally acknowledge his feeling about what has happened, and if possible, try to do something about the problem situation. If the situation is one which cannot, for the time being, be changed, he can decide to lump it and learn how to figure out a way of avoiding a similar occurrence in future.

When, however, the individual feels disturbed at point C, he is telling himself something like, "I can't stand what has happened to me! It's awful that it exists, and it absolutely shouldn't exist! I'm a worthless Joe for not doing something to avoid it happening, and you are a louse for inflicting me with it!"

Can you see why this second set of beliefs is irrational? This second set of beliefs is irrational because:

(1) it is rigid and absolutist;

(2) it cannot be empirically validated or disproven, because it consists of magical assumptions;

(3) it does not make sense;

(4) it leads to unpleasant emotional consequences which are quite unnecessary - for example, anxiety or depression; and

(5) instead of encouraging the individual to go back to the activating event at point A and try to change it (as his rational beliefs would), his irrational beliefs will interfere with and tend to block any constructive action he might be capable of taking, and may even help to make the situation worse.

Now let us analyse these irrational beliefs and see why they are unconfirmable. First, they represent a hypothesis that cannot be validated empirically. He can stand the unpleasant activating event at point A. He may never like it, and there is no reason why he should like it. But he can stand, he won't come apart at the seams!

Second, what does it mean to say that something is awful? How could one define it? It does not mean highly inconvenient or highly disadvantageous. Something more than that is implied. When applied to some stimulus, awful means more than 100% bad, more than 100% disadvantageous. But how can anything be more than 100% bad? Awful is a term carrying surplus meaning which has no definable empirical referent.

Third, by claiming that some unpleasant event in his life absolutely should not exist, the individual is issuing a God-like command that whatever he wants not to exist, absolutely should not exist. In effect, the individual is saying, "I am God, and I run the universe. So, what I say goes!" Obviously, this is another assertion that cannot be validated.

Finally, the individual thinks he is a worthless person because he failed to prevent the unfortunate activating event from happening. Now, he is denigrating himself for his inability to order the universe to run the way he wants it. "I must be able to see that obnoxious things do not happen and because I failed to do what I absolutely should have done, that means I'm no good." In addition, by demanding that some other person must do his bidding and behave differently from the way they actually did behave, the individual again makes another useless and self-damaging assumption.

The basic tenet of REBT, then, is that emotional disturbance is largely determined by the individual's irrational beliefs, and that these beliefs are irrational because they magically insist that some aspect or inference about the universe should, ought or must be different from the way it undoubtedly is. Although these irrational beliefs are connected with the activating events at point A, they bear no logical relation to these events. For they all boil down to the proposition, "Because I want something, it is not only desirable or preferable that it exists, but it must exist and it is awful when it doesn't!" No such proposition can ever be substantiated but, as therapists, you will come across literally myriads of people who devoutly cling to it, or to some equivalent variation of it. That being so, our previous assertion that humans are naturally crooked thinkers who find it easy to think in dogmatic, musturbatory ways, may no longer strike you as unusual.

To conclude this section, it is important to help clients to distinguish their rational beliefs about various activating events in their lives from their irrational beliefs, and to really understand why the difference is important. Help your clients to understand, until they need no prompting, that their unhealthy feelings stem from their strong dogmatic shoulds, oughts and musts, and that through challenging and uprooting these essentially magical notions they will be taking important steps to regaining emotional control over their lives. And if, at the same time, your clients work at, and practice acting against their deep-seated damaging behaviours, they can make headway against even their most stubborn self-defeating habits.

ACQUISITION AND PERPETUATION OF PSYCHOLOGICAL DISTURBANCE

REBT theory does not place much emphasis on an elaborate exposition of the way we acquire psychological disturbance. This is because of the REBT view that we have a profound biological tendency to think irrationally. However, REBT theory does acknowledge that environmental variables do contribute to our tendency to make ourselves disturbed by our own irrational belief system. Thus, if

I am treated harshly by my parents I am more likely to make demands about myself and demands about uncomfortable life conditions than I would be if my parents treated me well. However, this is by no means always the case and we have come across people who have had "a harsh upbringing" but have made less demands about themselves, others and life conditions than do some of our clients who have had much more favourable upbringings. Thus, REBT theory stresses that humans vary in their disturbability. The REBT theory of acquisition can be encapsulated in the view that we as humans are not made disturbed simply be our experiences, rather we bring our ability to disturb ourselves to these experiences.

REBT theory does, however, put forward a more elaborate view on the ways humans perpetuate their own disturbances. First, as previously stated, it argues that humans perpetuate their disturbances because they lack three major insights:

(1) psychological disturbance is primarily determined by musturbatory, and other rigid beliefs that people hold about themselves, others and the world;

(2) that people remain disturbed by reindoctrinating themselves in the present with these irrational beliefs; and

(3) that the only long-lasting way of overcoming disturbances is to work and practise against specific irrational beliefs and one's tendency to think and act irrationally.

REBT theory contends that a major reason why we perpetuate our psychological problems is because we adhere to a philosophy of low frustration tolerance. Thus, we tend to be short-range hedonists and to believe that we cannot stand discomfort, and even when we realise that we disturb ourselves with our beliefs in the present, we tend to think that just this awareness alone will lead us to overcoming our problems. Such individuals will do poorly in Rational Emotive Behaviour Therapy and other forms of psychotherapy too, because they steadfastly refuse to make themselves relatively uncomfortable now so that they can be more comfortable later. In particular, they tend to procrastinate putting into practice outside their therapy sessions what they learn inside their therapy sessions and will frequently come up with a variety of "good excuses" why they didn't do their homework assignments.

A further way that clients perpetuate their own disturbances is in making themselves disturbed (secondary disturbances) about their original disturbances. Thus, clients can make themselves anxious about their anxiety, guilty about their anger, depressed about their depression. ashamed about their own embarrassment etc, etc. Quite often, unless people tackle their secondary disturbances before their primary disturbances, they will impede themselves from overcoming their primary disturbances. Thus, unless a person accepts himself with his own anger problem instead of condemning himself for being angry, he will tend to get caught up in his self-blaming depression which will in itself, stop him from dealing with his primary anger problem.

Rational Emotive Behaviour Therapists agree with their psychoanalytic colleagues that we frequently employ defences to ward off threats to our ego and to our level of comfort. This will lead us to tend to deny that we have psychological problems when we most definitely do and may lead to us blaming others or life conditions for our problem. Such clients tend to resist the hypothesis of REBT that they largely make themselves disturbed because if they were to admit this then they would, for example, severely condemn themselves. Unless the ideas that underlie their defensiveness are uncovered and dealt with, then little progress is possible.

We also often perpetuate our own problems because we get some kind of pay-off from having such problems. Thus, we may get a lot of attention from others for having psychological problems which we are loath to do without, or our problems may protect us in our own minds from having more severe problems. When a person has a positive pay-off from having a psychological problem, such as attention from others, she is loath to work on overcoming her problems because she fears she may lose the attention which she craves from others. Here, note that in all probability she has an irrational belief about having such attention. When her psychological problem protects her in her own mind from a more severe problem then she will not be motivated to give up the emotional problem that she has at present, unless she is helped to also deal with the problem that she fears she might encounter. Finally, we often perpetuate our own problems because we make self-fulfilling prophecies. Thus, a man who has difficulties trusting women may, when he meets a new woman, be quite suspicious of her and indirectly discourage her from having warm intimate feelings towards him. This may lead to her leaving him which would confirm in his mind that women were not to be trusted. Unless clients who make self-fulfilling prophecies are encouraged to see the contribution that they themselves make to these prophecies, they are likely to perpetuate their relationship problems in the future.

THEORY OF THERAPEUTIC CHANGE

The REBT theory of therapeutic change is basically a simple one. It states that if clients are to overcome their emotional and behavioral problems, they need to

(a) recognise and acknowledge that they have a problem,

(b) overcome any secondary disturbance about the original problem,

(c) identify the irrational beliefs that underpin the problem(s),

(d) understand why their irrational beliefs are, in fact, irrational i.e. illogical, unable to be validated empirically, dogmatic and will give them poor results in life,

(e) realise why uprooting their magical, unsupportable beliefs and replacing them with rational realistic alternatives will give them more productive results,

(f) continue to challenge and dispute their irrational beliefs until they no longer carry conviction, and thereby strengthen their new rational philosophies,

(g) use a variety of cognitive, emotive, imaginal and behavioural assignments to strengthen their rational convictions and make them a fundamental part of their psychological make-up, as well as to seriously weaken their residual irrational notions,

(h) identify and overcome obstacles to therapeutic change using the same sequence as set out above, while still accepting themselves with their tendency to backslide and to construct such obstacles, and

(i) realise and act on the insight that, because they are fallible humans, they will on occasion, slip back into irrational ways of thinking, but that they can fully accept themselves with that tendency and continue to work and practise against it for the rest of their lives so that it no longer seriously troubles them.

SUMMARY

Rational Emotive Behaviour Therapy is based on a clear-cut theory of emotional health and disturbance, and the various techniques it employs are used in the light of that theory, and not in a random, or hit or miss manner. Theory and technique are closely integrated at every stage of the treatment process. REBT is hard-headed, scientific and empirically orientated and fosters the use of reason and the technology of emotional and behavioural re-education in the interests of human beings. REBT is avowedly humanistic, existentialist and unashamedly hedonistic. It makes growth and happiness the central concern of our intrapersonal and interpersonal life and its efforts are devoted to that end.

CHAPTER FOUR

KEY PRACTICAL ELEMENTS OF RATIONAL EMOTIVE BEHAVIOUR THERAPY

In this chapter we will outline key elements in the practice of Rational Emotive Behaviour Therapy.

Rational Emotive Behaviour Therapy is a structured problem-focused approach to psychotherapy. REBT therapists help their clients to identify their basic emotional problems and to deal with them one by one in a structured and problem-focused manner. REBT therapists consider their basic goal is to help their clients to identify the irrational beliefs that underpin their emotional disturbances and to challenge and change these beliefs in favour of rational beliefs. It is hypothesised that this will enable them to handle more constructively negative life situations and to lead more effective and fulfilling lives. REBT can therefore be seen as an educational form of psychotherapy and the relationship between therapist and client is one of an encouraging teacher helping his or her students to grow by thinking for themselves. Thus, REBT therapists favour adopting a Socratic-type dialogue with their clients in which the therapist encourages clients to question their own beliefs in an open-ended manner, but one which is directed to helping them to understand that while they cannot validate their irrational beliefs, they definitely can validate their rational ones. The aim of the Rational Emotive Behaviour Therapist is to show clients how to accomplish this and teach them how to use the methods employed to solve their own emotional problems throughout the rest of their lives.

THE GOALS OF REBT

REBT therapists agree with their Adlerian colleagues on the therapeutic value of therapist encouragement. Their basic attitude towards their clients is that with hard work and effort they can change their irrational beliefs, replace them with more rational, realistic beliefs, and eventually help themselves to overcome their emotional and behavioural problems. However, the key aspect here is the hard work and practice which clients are advised to put in if change in their basic philosophy is to be anything more than "skin deep". Working consistently against their engrained irrational philosophies in addition to acquiring more rational views of themselves and the world is of cardinal importance for clients in REBT. Given their hard-headed scientific outlook on psychotherapy and the process of therapeutic change, REBT therapists actively dissuade their clients from believing in quick, magical, painless and effortless cures. Instead, REBT therapists show their clients that therapeutic change is certainly possible, but that it does require hard and concerted and sustained effort from clients. For this and other reasons, REBT therapists encourage their clients to put up with personal discomfort and in certain ways encourage their clients to engage in challenging assignments, but not assignments that they would presently experience as overwhelming, in the service of therapeutic change.

Initially, Rational Emotive Behaviour Therapists encourage their clients to identify their primary and secondary emotional and behavioral problems and to work on overcoming them. Ideally, however, REBT therapists strive to enable their clients to make a profound philosophic change whereby they give up making demands on themselves, others and the world, and refrain from making absolutist ratings of themselves, others and life conditions. Clients are taught that while they may rate their deeds and performances, they cannot legitimately rate their "selves". The "self" is not a static entity but a process which undergoes frequent, or constant change throughout the life of the individual and therefore cannot be given any kind of global rating or score. The aim of such a profound philosophic change is to teach clients to accept themselves and others as fallible human beings, to habitually use the scientific method of testing their hypotheses about the beliefs they hold about themselves, others and the world, and by eliminating their dogmatic shoulds, oughts and musts, to minimally disturb themselves for the rest of their lives. While this ideal focus on encouraging clients to make a profound philosophic change is important, Rational Emotive Behaviour Therapists acknowledge that some clients may not be interested in making such a radical shift in their personality and they also recognise that many clients may not be able to embark on such a radical project. Thus, while REBT therapists will offer clients an opportunity to embark on a more radical restructuring of their personality, they are flexible in adjusting their goals to meet the goals of their clients.

This flexibility is also shown in their work with clients who are either unable or unwilling to work towards developing a new rational philosophy about specific elements of their lives. In such cases, REBT therapists will alter their therapeutic goals and encourage clients to make changes in their inferences, to work towards changing the negative events in their lives and to modify their behaviour so that they get some immediate benefit from the therapeutic process. However, REBT therapists do recognise that for the most part such clients are vulnerable to future disturbance because they have not addressed the core of their emotional and behavioral problems, i.e., the musturbatory and dogmatic demands that they make about themselves, others and the world. Thus, Rational Emotive Behaviour

Therapists are willing to compromise and do not dogmatically insist that their clients must always work towards addressing and overcoming their musturbatory cognitions. Wherever possible, however, REBT therapists strive to encourage their clients to internalise the three major REBT insights that were outlined in the section on acquisition and perpetuation of psychological disturbance. To reiterate, Rational Emotive Behaviour Therapists encourage their clients to acknowledge that past or present activating events do not cause their disturbed emotional and behavioural consequences; rather they strive to help their clients to acknowledge and internalise that it is their belief system about these activating events that "largely creates their disturbed feelings and behaviours". Rational Emotive Behaviour Therapists also encourage their clients to believe that irrespective of how they have disturbed themselves in the past, they now disturb themselves largely because they keep reindoctrinating themselves in the present with their irrational beliefs.

Finally, and most importantly, Rational Emotive Behaviour Therapists strive to help their clients to see that because they are human and very easily, and to some degree naturally, tend to disturb themselves because they find it easy to cling to their self-defeating thoughts, feelings and actions, nevertheless, they can largely (but not totally) overcome their disturbances in the long run, mainly by working hard and repeatedly both to dispute their irrational beliefs and to counteract the effects of these beliefs by strongly acting against them.

THE THERAPIST-CLIENT RELATIONSHIP

Albert Ellis has argued that the role of effective REBT therapists is akin to that of good teachers in that they strive to help their clients learn to become their own therapists once formal therapy sessions have ended. REBT does not dogmatically insist that any one kind of therapeutic relationship between therapist and client must be established; it thereby encourages therapeutic flexibility. Nevertheless, Rational Emotive Behaviour Therapists do tend to favour establishing certain therapeutic conditions and therapeutic styles with their clients.

Therapeutic conditions

One of the most important goals of Rational Emotive Behaviour Therapists is to encourage clients to accept themselves unconditionally as fallible human beings who often act self-defeatingly, but who are never essentially bad or good. As such, REBT therapists themselves strive to unconditionally accept their clients in the same way and will endeavour never to put their clients down or to dogmatically insist that their clients must behave in certain ways. However, this does not mean that Rational Emotive Behaviour Therapists do not bring to a client's attention aspects of the client's behaviour which are self-defeating and other-defeating. They, thus, strive to set up a therapeutic relationship where both therapist and client strive to accept themselves and the other person as fallible. The preferred REBT therapeutic relationship, therefore, is an egalitarian one where both participants are equal in their humanity, although unequal at the outset with respect to skills and expertise in personal problem solving.

Partly because of the egalitarian nature of the therapeutic relationship, REBT therapists strive to be as open as is therapeutically desirable and do not refrain from giving highly personal information about themselves should their clients ask for it, except when they judge that clients would use such information either against themselves or against their therapists. However, such openness and the self-disclosure which may well accompany it are encouraged for therapeutic purposes. Thus, when REBT therapists disclose that they have in the past experienced similar problems to their clients, it is not only to indicate that they are on an equal footing as humans with their clients but also to teach the clients how they, too, had to work to overcome these problems. Thus, in doing so, Rational Emotive Behaviour Therapists serve as good encouraging role models. Here the basic message is "I am human too, I have experienced similar problems to you in the past. I overcame them and this is how I overcame them; perhaps we can look at my experience and you can learn from this experience and take elements of it and apply this to your own problem solving work."

Ellis has often noted that emotional disturbance incorporates the attitude of taking life too seriously and thus REBT therapists tend to be appropriately humorous with most of their clients and will empathically and humorously demonstrate to their clients amusing aspects of the latter's dogmatic irrational beliefs and show them the therapeutic benefits of taking a serious, but not overly serious attitude towards life. In doing so it is important to realise that this is done within the spirit of an unconditional acceptance of their clients and that such humorous interventions are directed not at the clients themselves, but at their self-defeating thoughts, feelings and actions. However, it should be noted that some clients do not benefit from such humour and thus the principle of therapeutic flexibility applies, namely, varying one's style of intervention to maximise therapeutic relationships with specific clients.

The world of psychotherapy has been heavily influenced by the work of Carl Rogers, in particular his statements concerning the importance of certain core therapeutic conditions, i.e., therapist empathy, genuineness and unconditional positive regard. REBT therapists would agree with these, particularly those concerning unconditional acceptance and genuineness. With respect to empathy, Rational Emotive Behaviour Therapists not only believe in offering clients affective empathy, i.e., communicating that they understand how their clients feel, but also offering them philosophic empathy, i.e. showing them that they also understand the philosophies that underpin these feelings.

The one point where REBT therapists would disagree with a large majority of therapists from other therapeutic orientations concerns the role of therapist warmth in the counselling process. REBT therapists would argue that offering clients unconditional acceptance is likely to be of more importance than offering them undue counsellor warmth. For Rational Emotive Behaviour Therapists the latter has two major risks; first, therapist warmth may unwittingly reinforce clients' dire need for love and approval, two irrational beliefs which REBT therapists believe are at the core of much human disturbance; second, therapist warmth may also unwittingly reinforce the philosophy of low frustration tolerance that many clients already cling to. This is particularly the case if being warm means refraining from actively encouraging and in some cases, strongly pushing clients to involve themselves in uncomfortable experiences for the long term benefit of achieving therapeutic change.

Therapeutic style

Ellis (1979) recommends that Rational Emotive Behaviour Therapists adopt an active-directive style with most clients. He argues that such an active-directive style, particularly at the beginning of psychotherapy, is important in that it encourages clients to very quickly and efficiently go to the philosophic core of their emotional and behavioural problems. However, effective REBT therapists may vary their therapeutic style and adopt a variety of styles to fit the therapeutic requirements of different clients. Thus, they can adopt a formal therapeutic style with clients who believe that effective therapists are business-like and expert, and a more informal style with clients who would value interacting with a friendly, personally involved psychotherapist; and, last but not least, a tough no-nonsense approach with clients who would seem to benefit from such a therapeutic style. In addition, there maybe indications for different therapeutic styles with clients with different personality styles. Thus, Beutler (1983) has argued that it is important to avoid developing an overly friendly, emotionally charged style of interaction with "histrionic clients", an overly intellectual style with obsessive-compulsive clients and an overly directive style with clients whose sense of autonomy is easily threatened, as well as an overly active style with clients who very easily retreat into passivity. However, much more research is needed into this question of therapeutic flexibility with respect to counsellor style in REBT before any more definitive statements can be made on this issue. It is important to realise, as will be shown in Chapter 5, that the relationship between therapist and client often changes during the process of REBT, but particularly with respect to the active-directive aspects of the therapist's style. Thus, when REBT is effective, therapists encourage their clients to assume greater and greater responsibility for therapeutic change as therapy proceeds and consequently the therapist's level of directiveness fades. Here, Rational Emotive Behaviour Therapists often take a less directive prompting role, encouraging their clients to put into practice elements of the REBT problem solving method which they will have increasingly gained experience in employing during the early and middle phases of counselling.

EMPHASIS ON DISPUTING IRRATIONAL BELIEFS

We argued in the theoretical section of chapter 3 that REBT theory adheres to the principle of psychological interactionism, whereby it is held that beliefs, feelings and behaviours cannot be separated from one another, but in reality interact, often in quite complex ways. However, it is true that REBT therapists direct much of their therapeutic attention to helping clients to dispute their irrational beliefs, cognitively, emotively, imaginally and behaviourally. This emphasis on disputing irrational beliefs involves first, the ability to detect the presence of these irrational beliefs; second, the ability to discriminate them from rational beliefs; and third, an ability to engage in a process called debating, whereby clients are encouraged to debate with themselves the illogical, unempirical and inefficient aspects of their irrational beliefs. However, it should be noticed that although cognitive disputing is a central component of REBT, it is by no means the only defining feature of this approach to psychotherapy. We wish to underscore this because many critics, and indeed many researchers who have carried out empirical studies of Rational Emotive Behaviour Therapy, seem to equate REBT with its cognitive restructuring aspects. Thus, while the central core of REBT is teaching clients to dispute their irrational beliefs and to replace their irrational philosophies with rational philosophies, this is done in many different ways as will be shown below.

MULTIMODAL EMPHASIS

Rational Emotive Behaviour Therapists agree with multimodal therapists that it is important to take a multimodal approach to psychotherapy. Thus, REBT therapists encourage their clients to use many cognitive, emotive/evocative, imaginal and behavioural assignments to encourage them to work towards changing their irrational ideas. In addition, because it stresses the biological as well as the environmental and social sources of human disturbance, REBT frequently favours the use of medication where appropriate, and physical techniques, including nutrition, exercise and relaxation techniques, as an adjunct to the therapeutic process. However, such methods are used to encourage clients to work towards changing their irrational philosophies and are not used necessarily as an end in themselves.

SELECTIVE ECLECTICISM

Rational Emotive Behaviour Therapy is what I (WD) have called a theoretically consistent approach to eclecticism (Dryden, 1987). This means that REBT therapists can and do use a wide range of therapeutic techniques originated by therapists from other therapeutic schools. However, in doing so they do not accept the theoretical principles advocated by theorists from these other orientations; rather techniques are freely borrowed from other schools with the major purpose of encouraging clients to identify, challenge and change their irrational beliefs. As such, REBT de-emphasises the use of methods which discourage or impede clients from adopting a direct focus on changing their irrational ideologies. Thus it avoids, although not in any absolute sense, using the following:

(a) procedures that help people become dependent, e.g., the creation of a transference neurosis and the use of therapist warmth as a strong reinforcer;

(b) procedures that encourage clients to become more gullible and suggestible, e.g., certain kinds of Pollyannish positive thinking methods;

(c) procedures that are long-winded and inefficient, e.g., free association and other psychoanalytic methods that discourage clients from focusing on their irrational beliefs;

(d) procedures that help people to feel better in the short term rather than to get better in the long term, e.g., some experiential techniques like getting in touch with and fully expressing one's feelings;

(e) procedures that have dubious validity and that have not received empirical support from research studies even though proponents claim great therapeutic success for these procedures (e.g., neurolinguistic programming); and

(f) procedures that include anti-scientific and mystical philosophies (e.g., faith healing and mysticism) and procedures that appear to be harmful to a variety of clients, e.g., encouraging clients as in primal therapy, to scream and shout and to explosively express their angry feelings.

It should be noted, however, that REBT therapists may use some of these techniques for specific purposes. For example, using experiential techniques to help people to identify emotions prior to encouraging them to identify the irrational beliefs that underpin these emotions; using therapist warmth in the case of severe depression where the fact that a therapist may show that he is tremendously caring and concerned, may get through to such a depressed individual. In addition, Ellis (1985) has argued that he may even be prepared to use some of these inefficient techniques where all else fails with given clients.

THE IMPORTANCE OF HOMEWORK

Most Rational Emotive Behaviour Therapists see their clients for one hour a week. Thus, they do not see their clients for the remaining 167 hours in the week. This is a salutary reminder to those who claim that what goes on within the therapy session is more important than what goes on between therapy sessions. Ellis has always argued right from REBT's inception that clients who put into practice between sessions what they have learned within sessions will do much better in therapy than clients who steadfastly refuse to act on what they have learnt in therapy. Thus, for Rational Emotive Behaviour Therapists, encouraging clients to execute properly negotiated and well-designed homework assignments is considered to be a central part of the counselling process. Indeed, Ellis (1983) and Persons, Burns and Perloff (1988) have reported empirical data to suggest that clients who carry out homework assignments in cognitively-orientated approaches to psychotherapy achieve a better outcome than clients who do not execute such assignments. Therefore, effective REBT therapists pay a lot of attention to the homework variable in therapy and spend time discussing why this is a central part of the therapeutic process with clients and devote sufficient time to adequately negotiating such assignments with their clients. In particular, they pay specific attention to factors which may discourage clients from successfully carrying out homework assignments and strive to trouble-shoot such obstacles to psychotherapeutic change.

CONFRONTING AND OVERCOMING OBSTACLES TO CHANGE

We mentioned directly above that an important aspect of Rational Emotive Behaviour Therapy is identifying and overcoming obstacles to therapeutic change that may arise when clients strive to execute homework assignments. However, obstacles to change pervade the entire therapy process (Ellis, 1985; Neenan & Dryden, 1996) and a feature of REBT therapy is the recognition that such obstacles will occur and that a co-operative exploration between therapist and client concerning the nature of these obstacles, and the irrational beliefs that underpin them, is required as therapist and client attempt to overcome these obstacles so that they do not unduly interfere with the nature of therapeutic change. Obstacles to change can also occur within the therapy relationship; thus it may be that the particular match between therapist and client is not a good one and that the best way of handling this may be a judicious referral to a different REBT therapist.

Also it has to be acknowledged that some clients do not find REBT therapy a helpful therapeutic method and may well do better with a different approach to psychotherapy. This is because the ideas central to REBT - namely that one's emotional disturbance is determined by one's presently held irrational beliefs - and the theory of therapeutic change - specifically, that one has to work and practice to overcome one's emotional and behavioural problems - are at variance with the beliefs of the client, and no amount of therapist intervention may change the client's mind on these points. Again, a judicious referral to a therapist from a different therapy school may be indicated. However, relationship obstacles to change can occur because the therapist has unwittingly adopted a therapeutic style which implicitly reinforces the client's difficulties. Thus, the therapist may be offering the client too much warmth and inadvertently reinforcing the client's needs for approval or the therapist may adopt an overly directive style of interaction which encourages an already passive client to become more passive in therapy and in life. It is important for therapists to monitor their style of participation and to continually ask themselves whether or not their therapeutic style is encouraging or discouraging their clients from changing.

The second source of obstacles to more lasting therapeutic change resides in clients themselves, and this issue of helping clients maintain their therapeutic gains will be dealt with in chapter 5. However, for present purposes it should be noticed that clients may have irrational beliefs about certain aspects of the Rational Emotive Behaviour Therapy process which may discourage them from changing In particular, they may well have a philosophy of low frustration tolerance towards taking major responsibility for effecting their own improvement. Thus, they may believe that they should not be expected to work hard in therapy and that doing so is too difficult and too uncomfortable. It is important that REBT therapists encourage their clients to identify, challenge and change, such change-impending philosophies if clients are going to benefit in the long term from REBT.

Rational Emotive Behaviour Therapists are by no means immune from their own self-defeating beliefs which may well contribute to discouraging clients from changing. Thus, Ellis (1985) has outlined five major irrational beliefs that therapists may hold that may serve as obstacles to client change:

(1) I have to be successful with all of my clients practically all of the time.

(2) I must be an outstanding therapist, clearly better than other therapists that I know or hear about.

(3) I have to be greatly respected and loved by all my clients.

(4) Since I am doing my best and working so hard as a therapist, my clients should be equally hard working and responsible, should listen to me carefully and should always push themselves to change.

(5) Because I'm a person in my own right, I must be able to enjoy myself during therapy sessions and to use these sessions to solve my personal problems as much as to help my clients with their difficulties.

The presence of these beliefs may lead therapists to back off from encouraging clients to change when this is appropriate and desirable, or to become inappropriately involved with their clients in a manner that sidetracks Rational Emotive Behaviour Therapy from its problem-solving focus. It is thus important for REBT therapists to regularly monitor their work. They should be prepared to fully accept themselves if and when they discover that they are side-tracking the therapy process so that they can more effectively identify the irrational beliefs that underpin such sidetracking; and they had better consult frequently with their supervisors who may be able to spot sidetracking instances that they (the therapists) have not yet identified and which may indicate that their own irrational beliefs have come to the fore and are serving as an obstacle to client change.

FORCE AND ENERGY IN THERAPEUTIC CHANGE

The theory of REBT holds that when clients are emotionally disturbed they tend to cling very forcefully and energetically to their main irrational beliefs, and that even when they have "insight" into these beliefs they may still strongly believe them and refuse to give them up. In such circumstances, Rational Emotive Behaviour Therapists are not loathe to engage in very forceful and energetic disputing of their clients' irrationalities and to encourage their clients to intervene very forcefully, vividly and energetically when they are disputing their own irrational beliefs. Thus, force and energy can be brought to a whole host of cognitive, imaginal and behavioural assignments and serve to remind critics that Rational Emotive Behaviour Therapy stresses the emotive aspects of psychotherapy and can bring passion to the counselling process. Indeed, REBT therapists often encourage their clients to develop a passion for working forcefully and energetically to give up these beliefs. Without this focus on force and energy, clients may well very weakly and insipidly challenge their irrational beliefs and will thus experience very little benefit.

No discussion of the key elements in REBT practice would be complete without taking a look at what kinds of personality characteristics are associated with effective REBT therapists. Since this important matter deserves a chapter to itself, the reader is referred to chapter eight.

In this chapter we have outlined the basic principles of Rational Emotive Behaviour Therapy. In particular, we have discussed the theory that underpins the practice of REBT and the key elements of this approach to therapy in action. In the next chapter we will consider the REBT process of change and its treatment sequence.

CHAPTER FIVE

THE PROCESS OF CHANGE AND THE REBT TREATMENT SEQUENCE

THE PROCESS OF CHANGE

We will now briefly outline a typical sequence in the process of Rational Emotive Behaviour Therapy. At the beginning of therapy, therapists will encourage clients to identify their major emotional problems and will communicate understanding of these problems from the clients' point of view. In the process of doing so, clients are helped to see that REBT is a structured, problem-focused approach to psychotherapy and personality change and one, moreover, which requires clients to work to achieve therapeutic change. Problems are taken one by one, and once clients have identified their problems, these are assessed with special reference to the irrational beliefs which the clients, with the aid of their therapists, have targeted for change. Therapists help their clients to question these beliefs and in later sessions to replace the irrational beliefs with more rational beliefs and to put these into practice to strengthen them and weaken their disturbance-creating irrational beliefs. REBT rarely goes smoothly, and various obstacles to change do occur throughout the process. Here clients and therapists work together to identify such obstacles, and various modifications in therapeutic style, speed and focus are made as a result. In addition, clients' irrational beliefs about the process of therapy and about the process of change are targeted for discussion and change during this process.

THE REBT TREATMENT SEQUENCE

We will now take you through the major steps of the REBT sequence and outline the 13 steps that we have identified as comprising this sequence.

Step 1: Ask for a problem

After you have greeted your client (in this case female), help her to discuss her reasons for coming for therapy, and to talk about her problems in a fairly open-ended manner, and show empathic understanding of her position. Then ask her for a specific problem to work on. This might be the client's major problem or the problem which she wishes to start on first.

Step 2: Define and agree the target problem

It is important for you and your client to have a common understanding of what this particular problem is, and a shared understanding that this problem will be the focus for initial therapeutic exploration. The more specifically you can help your client to identify the nature of the problem, the more likely it is that you will then be successful in carrying out an assessment of this problem. This is accomplished by using the ABC framework of REBT, where A equals the activating event, or the client's inference about this event; B stands for the client's belief about the event; and C stands for the client's emotional and behavioural consequences of holding the belief at B. You can make this clear to the client by taking a specific example of her problem.

Step 3: Assess C

The first part of the REBT treatment sequence involves the assessment of C - the client's emotions and behaviour. It is important at this stage that you help her to focus on an unhealthy negative emotion, such as demanding anger, depression, anxiety or feelings of hurt, etc. You would also be advised to be on the look-out for self-defeating actions or behaviour, such as procrastination, addictions, and so on. However, clients who report experiencing concern, or sadness in response to a loss, annoyance or some other kind of disappointment, and who are taking effective action and leading self-disciplined lives, are in fact handling themselves constructively. This follows from the observation that it is generally regarded as unrealistic for human beings to have neutral or positive feelings about negative events in their lives. Thus, it is important at this point to help your client to identify a self-defeating negative emotion, not a constructive negative emotion. At this step, you can also assess your client's motivation to change her unhealthy negative emotion and encourage her to strive towards experiencing the more constructive negative emotion. This, however, can be done elsewhere in the assessment part of the sequence (i.e., between steps 3 and 6).

Step 4: Assess A

Once you have clarified what C is, you are now in a position to find out what your client specifically was disturbed about in the actual example you are assessing. If you recall from the Finger Pointing Exercise in chapter 1, the objective reality was that I (WD) was walking around the circle in front of the group, my hand raised in the air. That was the reality. Different workshop participants focused on different aspects of the situation. Some of them, for example, focused their attention on their own inferences of the situation, such as that I was acting in an unfair manner. Others took the view that something threatening would happen as a result of my walking around in this manner. Consequently, it is important to realise that when you assess A, you are not only trying to assess the objective situation which your client was in, but the subjective aspects of that situation. This involves looking for your client's inferences about A. Your major task here is to identify the most relevant inference involved, the particular inference which triggered the client's irrational beliefs which in turn led to her disturbed feelings or behaviours at C. In REBT, this is called the critical A.

Step 5: Determine the presence of secondary emotional problems and assess if necessary

It often transpires that clients have secondary emotional problems about their original emotional problems. For example, clients can often feel guilty about their anger, ashamed about their depression, anxious about their anxiety, guilty about their procrastination, etc. Therefore, at this point in the process, or earlier if appropriate, it is important to determine whether or not your client does have a secondary emotional problem about her primary emotional problem. If she does have a secondary problem, then it is important to target this problem for treatment first before proceeding to deal with the primary problem if you consider that the secondary problem is going to significantly interfere with your work on the primary problem. So, if your client is feeling ashamed about her anger, for example, then those feelings of shame may interfere with and possibly block effective work on helping her overcome her anger and thus shame (the secondary emotional problem) would be dealt with first in this case.

Step 6: Teach the iB-C connection

Whether you are proceeding with your client's primary emotional problem or whether you have switched and are now in the process of assessing a secondary emotional problem, the next stage in the REBT treatment sequence is to help the client to understand the connection between unhealthy negative emotions and irrational beliefs (iBs). Specifically, strive to help your client to understand that these emotions do not stem from activating events or inferences of these events, but from irrational beliefs about these events or inferences. If you fail to do this, your client will be puzzled by your emphasis on assessing her irrational beliefs. It is important, therefore, to bring out the connection between the iBs and Cs at the right stage in the REBT treatment sequence.

Step 7: Assess irrational beliefs

Assuming that you have successfully assessed A and C, you are now in a position to help your client to identify the specific irrational beliefs that she has about the event or situation that brought about her problem at C. In particular, be on the lookout for the following:

(a) *Demandingness*

Here your client will be making absolute demands about A in the form of 'musts', 'shoulds', 'oughts'. 'have to's', etc.

(b) *Awfulising*

Here, your client will be saying things like, "it's awful, horrible or terrible that A occurred" or that "it is the end of the world."

(c) *Low Frustration Tolerance*

Help your client to look out for irrational beliefs indicative of low frustration tolerance, or an attitude of "I can't stand it". Your client will frequently say something was intolerable, or unbearable, or too hard to put up with, etc.

(d) *Statements of damnation*

Under this heading you will hear your client making global negative evaluations of herself, other people and/or the life conditions she is living under. These global statements of evaluation can be extreme, such as, "I am a rotten person", or they may be less extreme but still basically irrational and unsupportable because they involve a total or global evaluation of the self - which is, in reality, far too complex to be given a rating, or indeed, as you will see later, any kind of rating whatever. Thus, your client may, to use a less extreme example, insist that she is less worthy or less lovable as a result of what happened at A. This is still a global kind of rating, however, and if it occurs you will note it for later discussion.

Step 8: Connect your client's irrational beliefs with her C's

Before proceeding to encourage your client to challenge her irrational beliefs, it is important, first of all, help her see the connection between her specific irrational beliefs and the disturbed negative emotions and self-defeating behaviours at point

C. If this is not done, or not done adequately, your client will not understand why you will soon be proceeding to encourage her to question her irrational beliefs. Even if you discussed the general connection between iB and C at Step 6, you still need to help your client to understand the specific connection between irrational beliefs and C at Step 8.

Step 9: Dispute irrational beliefs

The major goals of disputing at this point in the REBT treatment process is to encourage your client to understand that her irrational beliefs are unproductive, that is, that they lead to self-defeating emotions and are illogical and inconsistent with reality. Moreover, these irrational beliefs cannot be supported by any factual evidence or scientific reasoning. By contrast, rational alternatives to these beliefs are productive, logical, consistent with reality and self-helping. They will not get the client into trouble, but instead help her to achieve her goals in life with the minimum of emotional and behavioural upsets. More specifically, the goals of disputing are to help your client to understand the following:

(1) *Musts:* That there is no evidence in support of her absolute demands, while evidence does exist for her preferences.

(2) *Awfulising*: That what your client has defined as awful that is, more than 100% bad, cannot be upheld and that in reality it will lie within a scale of badness from 0 - 99.99%. Only one thing could be regarded as totally bad, and that is death itself; but even that is debatable since it is possible to regard death as preferable to dying slowly in excruciating agony with no hope whatever of relief. Often when you are helping your client to understand that if she rates something as more than 100% bad, she is really saying that nothing else in the world could possibly be worse. Once your client can see that this is absurd, she can more readily accept that her evaluation is greatly exaggerated.

(3) *Low frustration tolerance*: That your client can always stand what she thinks she can't stand, and can be reasonably happy, although not as happy as she would be if the difficult situation she has outlined at point A changed for the better.

(4) *Damnation or making global negative ratings of self, others or the world:* That this cannot legitimately be done because humans are human, that is, fallible beings, and are not in any way damnable no matter what they do or don't do. Further, human beings are too complex to be given a single global rating which completely summarises their total being. Statements like "I am   worthless", for

example, mean that I am totally without worth or value to myself or to anybody else and possess no redeeming features whatever. How could this ever be substantiated? Obviously, it couldn't. Similarly, the world, too, is not damnable and contains a mixture of good, bad and other complex aspects which cannot possibly be given some kind of a global rating. Once you can get your client to understand and accept this, she will become less inclined to deify or devilify herself or others and more able to accept herself and others as fallible, but non-damnable human beings.

At the end of Step 9, if you have been successful in helping your client to dispute her irrational beliefs, you will perceive a new awareness in your client of the lack of any real evidence to support her previously held irrational beliefs and an acceptance of these beliefs as illogical and both self-and-relationship-defeating. At the same time, you will observe the gradual emergence of the client's appreciation of why the new rational beliefs are logical reality-based and self-helping, as well as potentially relationship-enhancing with others. A word of caution, however. Your client's newly acquired rational beliefs are unlikely to become deep, solid convictions overnight. She may say things like, "I understand what you are saying, and I think I believe it, but I don't feel it in my gut." It takes time for your client's new beliefs about herself and the world to sink in, so to speak, and to become an integral part of her psychological make-up. For that reason, the remaining steps in the REBT treatment process are devised to help your client to internalise her rational beliefs to the point that she can say with conviction, "Yes, I now understand what you are saying in my gut as well as in my head and I can now act on this rational understanding".

Step 10: Prepare your client to deepen her conviction in her rational beliefs

At this point, before you encourage your client to put into practice her new learning, it is important to help her understand that long term therapeutic change does involve a good deal of hard work on her part if she is ever going to deepen her new rational convictions to the point that they become virtually a new rational philosophy of living.

Step 11: Encourage your client to put her learning into practice

You are now in a position to help your client put into practice a variety of cognitive, emotive, imagery and behavioral assignments. These are discussed with your client and she plays an active role in choosing assignments that are most relevant for her. At this point we would like to carry out two exercises with you to give you an opportunity to experience for yourselves what type of assignments are used in Rational Emotive Behaviour Therapy. But for a fuller discussion of the variety of assignments that are used, consult Dryden & Yankura (1993) and Ellis & Dryden (1997).

RATIONAL-EMOTIVE IMAGERY

Rational-emotive imagery is an imagery exercise designed to help clients to gain practice at changing their unhealthy negative emotions to more healthy negative emotions by changing their irrational beliefs to rational beliefs. Take one of your negative self-defeating emotions, such as anger, depression or feelings of hurt and vividly imagine the situation in which you experience these feelings. Close your eyes and clearly imagine the event in which you experienced those feelings and allow yourself to keenly feel the emotion concerned. Then, while still imagining the event as clearly and as vividly as you can, change your negative self-defeating emotion to one which is more constructive, but still negative. For example, if you are feeling damningly angry, change that feeling to non-damning anger or annoyance; if you are feeling depressed, change that to sadness; if anxious, change your anxiety to concern; and if you are feeling hurt, change your feeling of hurt to one of disappointment. Keep trying until you actually do change your self-defeating negative emotion to a constructive negative emotion.

Once you have succeeded, open your eyes and ask yourself exactly what beliefs you changed to bring about your change in feeling. Suppose you experienced damning anger; you would have changed that to non-damning anger or annoyance by changing your irrational beliefs which created the damning anger. What were these beliefs? A fairly common one is, "The other person absolutely should not have treated me in that unfair manner, especially after all I've done for him!" If you changed your damning anger to non-damning anger or annoyance, you probably told yourself something like, "While I don't like the other person's behaviour, there's no reason why he absolutely should not have treated me badly. I would much prefer the other person to treat me more considerately, and maybe I can persuade him to do so. But angrily damning him for his behaviour will only give me a pain in the gut and will probably induce him to be just as inconsiderate in the future!"

A different version of rational-emotive imagery involves you deliberately changing your beliefs while you are experiencing your self-defeating feeling in order to bring about a change in that feeling. Thus, vividly imagine the event in which you experienced your self-defeating negative feeling, identify your irrational demands creating the feeling and deliberately change those demands to wishes or preferences, while still vividly imagining the event. If you were feeling anxious, for example, because you were demanding that a particular threatening event must not happen, continue imagining that the feared event might happen, but this time convince yourself that you would definitely prefer that the event didn't occur, but that there is no reason why it must not; and if it does occur, that might be unfortunate but it isn't terrible and you can stand it.

A SHAME-ATTACKING EXERCISE

Shame-attacking exercises are designed to help clients to act in what they consider to be a "shameful" manner in public while gaining practice at accepting themselves for doing so, but not putting themselves down for it. So, select some kind of behaviour, which if you performed in public would probably earn you scorn and lead you to experience shame for acting in that manner. However, make sure that your planned exercise is one which is unlikely to harm you or cause unnecessary alarm to others. We don't want you to land up in prison or lose your job! Some typical behaviours might be: wearing outlandish clothes which will attract the criticism of other people; acting in an inappropriate or inept manner in public, by going into a newsagent's shop, for example, and asking them if they sell bedroom suites; or asking a stranger for directions to the street along which you are actually walking. In other words, a shame-attacking exercise involves socially inappropriate behaviour and the aim of the exercise is to show the participant that no matter how socially inept or foolish his or her behaviour may appear to others, they can still accept themselves in the face of public scorn or criticism without in any way downing themselves for their behaviour.

First, look for the irrational belief behind the 'shame' of acting in the proposed manner; for example, the belief that other people will think you are something of an idiot and laugh at you and that you couldn't stand the disapproval of others. When you do your shame-attacking exercise, it is important that you not only act in a socially inappropriate manner, but that you also at the same time dispute your irrational belief behind your feeling of shame. What are you telling yourself when someone notices your behaviour and either laughs at you, or tells you off?. Is the criticism of others going to kill you, or is it merely unfortunate? Once you convince yourself that a foolish act cannot make you a foolish person but merely a person who acts foolishly, you can accept yourself as an imperfect human being who occasionally behaves stupidly or inappropriately but in no way is less worthy for doing so. Stay in the "shameful" situation until you have changed your feelings of shame to those of disappointment, irritation, or whatever other emotion is appropriate in the situation. One further word of advice. When you do your shame-attacking exercise do not look away from others. Look at them directly in the eye. This is because gaze avoidance reduces your feelings of shame. We want you to eliminate shame by attacking the irrational beliefs that underpin this emotion rather than by non-belief change methods.

Step 12: Check the homework assignment

The next step in the REBT treatment sequence is for you to check your client's homework assignment. This may have been a shame-attacking exercise, or some other activity which your client has been reluctant to face because of some emotional block arising from irrational beliefs concerning the situation. It is important to ascertain if she faced the situation that she agreed to face and whether or not she changed her irrational beliefs in the process of doing so. If the assignment was not carried out satisfactorily, reassign the task after verifying whether your client's failure was due to the continuing existence in her mind of those irrational beliefs which the exercise was designed to undermine in the first place. Should that turn out to be the case, once more invite your client to identify and challenge the irrational beliefs which sidetracked her from carrying out the assigned task. When this has been done, reassign the task and monitor the result.

Step 13: Facilitate the working through process

Once your client has achieved a measure of success in changing some of her irrational beliefs by successfully executing the relevant homework assignments, go on from there to help your client to develop other assignments designed to help her gain experience in behaving in accordance with her emerging new rational philosophy. Thus, if your client has successfully challenged the irrational beliefs concerning public disapproval in social situations, help her to maximise her gains by designing assignments aimed at helping her to recognise and dispute any irrational beliefs she might have about disapproval in other situations such as work relations with colleagues or personal relations with significant others. Your aim is not only to help your client to recognise and rip up her irrational beliefs about whatever situation or problem is currently troubling her, but also to show her how to generalise her new learning to any future problem which she might experience. Once your client has gained experience and achieved success at challenging and disputing the irrational beliefs underlying one particular problem, she is more likely to take on greater responsibility for initiating the REBT sequence with other problems. At the end of Rational Emotive Behaviour Therapy, the degree of success achieved by both you and your client may be gauged by the extent to which she demonstrates the ability to live a more satisfying life with few, if any, of the emotional hangups with which she began therapy originally.

However even the brightest and most enthusiastic of clients may, on occasion, slip back into their old self-defeating ways. The answer? Back to the basics you go! It is on occasions like this, that you will see the emergence of what we referred to previously as secondary problems. Here, your client upsets herself because she has experienced some kind of a relapse. For example, your client may have felt guilty over some act of commission or omission and she is now denigrating herself for feeling guilty. "How stupid of me to upset myself again, and after all I've learned about REBT! Boy, what a dumbo that makes me!"

If your client reports a relapse, consider it as normal, as par for the course. In any case, nobody is completely rational. We can think, feel and behave rationally most of the time and rarely upset ourselves over the various hassles and problems of living in a complex world. But can we realistically expect to be like that all of the time? Hardly! Assure your client, therefore, that to take two steps forward then one step back, is the common experience. Don't waste time commiserating with your client. Instead, repeat the 13 step REBT sequence. Help your client to understand that staying emotionally healthy doesn't come about automatically, but requires continuous work and practice before the REBT philosophy she has been trying hard to assimilate actually becomes an integral part of her life.

Show your client that there is no reason why she absolutely must not feel ashamed or dejected because some old emotional problem has returned to plague her. Encourage her to accept that this is normal, a natural part of our human fallibility. Emphasise (once more) that we all have innate tendencies to think in absolutistic, musturbatory ways and that we are all naturally crooked thinkers; it comes easy to us! At this point retrace your steps and use the ABC framework to re-orient your client back to the task of disputing her irrational beliefs. Your client already knows that her previous problem(s) became established through her habitually thinking thoughts that created it. OK. So, go after those irrational beliefs with your client. Get your client to identify, challenge and dispute them until she is thoroughly convinced of their falseness. Encourage her to look for variations of the main irrational beliefs and to understand why they are irrational and cannot be accepted as true, regardless of what form they are presented in. Help your client to keep looking, and looking, for her absolutistic demands upon herself and others, the shoulds, oughts and musts, and to replace them with flexible, non-dogmatic desires and preferences.

Finally, stress the importance, once more, of your client acting against her irrational beliefs until she becomes comfortable doing what she was already unrealistically afraid to try. Show your client how she can put muscle into her newly acquired REBT philosophy by means of self-management techniques, rational-emotive imagery exercises and shame-attacking exercises until she convinces herself that she really can make headway against even her most stubborn self-defeating beliefs and habits. When your client reaches the stage where she can easily recognise and distinguish her healthy from her unhealthy negative feelings, understand why the difference is important, and demonstrate not only that she can uproot these shoulds, oughts and musts which underlie her self-defeating feelings, but also that she can replace these with rational beliefs, you may assume that your client is well on her way to regaining effective emotional control of her life.

CHAPTER SIX

RATIONAL EMOTIVE BEHAVIOUR THERAPY IN ACTION: TRANSCRIPT OF ALBERT ELLIS WITH FIONA

The following is a transcript of a demonstration therapy session conducted by Albert Ellis. From time to time we shall stop the tape as it were to comment on what is happening and to explain the significance of certain interesting features of Ellis's interventions. Throughout, we shall designate the responses of therapist and client respectively as T1, T2..... etc and C1, C2..... etc.

T1 Fiona, what problem would you like to talk about today?

C1 Actually I would like to just express my feelings about myself and what is going on in my life that I can't seem to cope with.

T2 Yeah sure, especially what you can't seem to cope with and then I'll see if we can give you some ideas on how to cope with what you presumably can't cope with.

C2 That would be terrific. Um.... basically I would say my whole life has been a roller-coaster but it's much heavier at this point in my life.... my feelings of anger towards the world and with that anger also goes a feeling of self-pity and despair. It kind of changes from that, in other words I don't want to feel angry and I don't know how to express my anger so I hold it inside of me and I take it and turn it around and hurt myself.

T3 Yeah, well let me just see if I understand that.... (Fiona: OK).... I think you are saying that you have two feelings - one is that you feel very angry and you don't like that feeling, you don't want to feel that way but then you are also saying you feel like expressing the anger and you believe that if you express it, you will get it out and then it will go, but, since you don't express it, you then may put yourself down for not expressing it - is that correct?

C3 Yes, so I'm angry at myself for not expressing it but I am also terrified of feeling and showing that anger because I don't know if I can control it ... (Ellis: Right) ... Anger frightens me. It's been part of my life .... I can't even handle yelling, it's just terrifying, it's hurt my whole life, it's hurt my marriages, my relationships with friends and family and .... I would like to have a healthy attitude in terms of my feelings with anger because I end up hurting myself all the time .... (Ellis: Right) .... It doesn't accomplish anything in my life .... (Ellis: Right) .... and it also reflects itself in my professional life. I can't seem to stay in one career and work at something where I can .... at my age, I'm 36, I want to feel successful, I want to have a successful life .... and really....

T4   But as I see it, and again you correct me if I'm wrong, you have two levels: first the anger, which you are afraid might be really terrific and outstanding and overwhelm you, but then also you are terrified about the anger .... (Fiona: Absolutely) .... Because it knocks you off - is that right? .... (Fiona: Mm hmm) Why don't we start with the second one then we'll get back to the anger itself, but just let's talk about first, if you want to, the terror about the anger. Do you want to start there and then we'll get back to the anger itself?

[From what he has heard so far, it appears to Ellis that Fiona has a secondary problem - her terror of expressing her anger because she feels she can't handle it. Ellis appears to have decided that it would be more productive to work on the secondary problem first, as is common in REBT, on the grounds that resolving the secondary problem will facilitate a resolution of the primary problem. However, Ellis first asks Fiona if she agrees to proceeding in this way.]

C4   The terror, since I've never been angry in my life, I can only assume what I am going to feel and that is out of control.

[Having obtained Fiona's agreement to tackling the secondary problem first, Ellis proceeds to do so.]

T5   Well let's just assume the worst there, that you did, that you let yourself go on one occasion or a few occasions and you felt out of control, let's just suppose that, you got beyond yourself and your felt out of control. Now what are you afraid would then happen? Can you picture that out of controlledness and ....?

C5   The, I see myself shaking, I see myself.... quivering. I see myself possibly killing - I don't know, it gets.... I can't go that far with it.... (Ellis: Right).... and I also see someone not liking me.

T6   Right. Alright then let's just picture yourself shaking and quivering and feeling really murderous and somebody watching you or several people watching you and not liking you. Now, why would that be horrible if that were so, because we're deliberately now assuming the worst so to get you to see that even if you did express this anger it might not be the end of the world, but why would that be horrible if you expressed it, you got out of control and somebody or several people really disliked you?

[Observe here how Ellis accurately paraphrases what Fiona has said, including her inference that people wouldn't like her if she expressed her anger to them. That last bit might strike some people as relatively unimportant. After all, nobody enjoys being the recipient of someone else's anger. However, Ellis senses that Fiona's expressed inference that someone might not like her if she lost control and let go of her anger could be significant, so he picks up this point and proceeds to explore it. Note also that Ellis encourages Fiona to assume temporarily that her inference at A is true. This is a typical REBT strategy and its main purpose is to identify the client's irrational belief.]

C6   I really wouldn't know how to handle it, I really wouldn't know how to.... I can't handle people not liking me, it's....

T7   Because you feel what? When people don't like you, what's your own feeling? Let's suppose people don't like you and that's specially because you are really out of control, you're angry, then how do you feel...?

C7   Then I feel they'll see me for who I am.

T8   And let's suppose now that....

C8   They're seeing a horrible person.

T9   All right, now you prove to me that you are a horrible person if you're out of control and if people don't like you, how does that make you a horrible person?

C9   It's hard to answer that you know.... that's the whole problem.

[At this point, Ellis has identified Fiona's secondary problem as low self-acceptance: they're seeing a horrible person, which is a form of negative self-evaluation. He assumes that Fiona means that she thinks that she is a horrible person and goes on to challenge this belief.]

T10 I know, but if we can get you to see that you are not a horrible person - you are a person who is acting, we'll say badly, very angrily out of control and unloved in this instance, then we'll solve maybe the most important part of your whole problem. But just think about that, you're out of control and people are hating you for being out of control. They are thinking you're a twerp, you're no good and you're really an impossible person. Now how does that make you no good?

[Notice how the focus of the session has shifted from a discussion of Fiona's anger to her irrational belief that she is a horrible person if she loses control and expresses her anger at people. Notice also how Ellis begins to challenge this irrational belief.]

C10 Well actually it doesn't, it probably is the reverse, it would be good for me to be that way because it's healthy.

[At C10, on the face of it, Fiona thinks it might be healthy for her if she expressed her anger. Ellis quickly dispells this apparent misconception.]

T11 Well, you're thinking that's healthy, that doesn't have to be....

C11 Healthy, meaning I can't be a smiling, lovely person all the time.

[Fiona seems to have confused expressing anger with being assertive. Ellis picks up this point.]

T12 That's right. I don't think personally from our standpoint in Rational Emotive Behaviour Therapy that it's healthy to be angry, but it's healthy to be assertive, to be yourself... (Fiona: That's it exactly).... and if you were yourself and.... (Fiona: I'd feel good, I'd feel damned good)....Right, but now let's suppose you're not just assertive, you're horribly angry... (Fiona: I'm horribly angry).... You're getting people upset about it. Now again why would you have to put you down - not the out of control down because that wouldn't be so good. Now why would you have to put you as a human down if that were so?

[Here Ellis tries to get Fiona to make the distinction between thinking badly of herself as a person, and disliking an aspect of her behaviour - her out-of-controlledness.]

C12 Because it would reinforce what I think of myself.

T13 And why do you think so badly of yourself?

C13 That goes back too long - it's too deep.... it's too deeply embedded in me.

T14 Well I don't happen to think so. In Rational Emotive Behaviour Therapy we say that it does go back and you probably felt this way right from the beginning - from age two, three or four because even then you had a certain implicit philosophy which you brought to any situation.... (Fiona: Correct).... and that philosophy, do you know what that probably was, even at two, three, four and five....?

C14 I was a brat.... (Ellis: Right).... I provoked my father who was an angry person....(Ellis: Right).... and only because I wanted him to show me his love.... (Ellis: Right).... but instead I didn't know how to handle him, I didn't understand what was going on, I would provoke him to get his attention and he would hit me.

T15 All right, but you see you first provoked him to show his love. Now your philosophy behind that in regard to your being loved, what do you think that might have been?

C15 My philosophy then was to get his love, his attention.... (Ellis: Right).... but it never worked that way.

T16 But was it just a desire or was it a need?

[Ellis suspects that Fiona's self-downing may spring from a failure to win love and/or approval for which she has a dire need.]

C16 It was a need.... (Ellis exaggerates: Ahhh!).... an absolute need.

T17 And that's what you brought to the situation at two, three, four, five, six. You had a dire need, necessity, for love and then you did everything - even acted brattily, did anything even against this father who was very angry himself. So your first philosophy that I see was a dire need for love, which incidentally I see you still having.... (Fiona: absolutely).... and that's why you did that. But then there was a second philosophy which was probably there too, along with the dire need for love, and I'm just going to talk about it now - and then you check me - that I have to act well, I have to do the right thing AND therefore be approved - is it possible that you've always had that kind of philosophy?

C17 Yeah I had to be the nice sweet little Fiona.... (Ellis: Right).... .... (Ellis: Right).... people would like me and think what a nice little girl.

T18 But do you see the contradiction right from the start?

C18 I was rebelling against....

T19 That's a little later, first I have to be myself and win love, and almost every child wants to win love and be approved especially by her father, mother and people like that, but instead of I'd like to, I have to. And then when I'm not loved I'll do almost anything because I have to do well and have to be loved and I'll even rebel. I need: 1) the attention, love, - but 2) I need to express myself even when it gets me into trouble - isn't that what you felt as a child? - and don't you still feel a lot of that conflict that....

C19 Absolutely. I mean I did the same provocation in my marriage.... (Ellis: Yeah?).... because I could not believe that this man really could love me and I had to test him all the time until he... er... he couldn't take it any longer.

T20 So we're right back to I need, I absolutely must have his love and then I will even go to extremes and test people.... (Fiona: it's very frightening).... and then when they fail the test and don't love you that much, how do you feel about them?

C20 Exactly; how do I feel about them?

T21 When you've tested your husband's love or your father's love and they failed and they didn't really love you as much as you thought they should....

C21 Then it actually.... what it was doing was reinforcing the fact that I'm not a good person.

T22 Ah, reinforcing in your philosophy.... (Fiona: Yes).... 'cos I must be loved and I must do well.

[Here Ellis raps his fist against his hand to emphasize the word "must".]

C22 He promised he would love me forever, my father supposedly should have loved me no matter what, and he didn't.

T23 Because he's my father?

C23 Because he's my father.

T24 Right, and my husband because he's my husband?

C24 Yes, - and because he promised me that he'd love me forever, but he didn't.

T25 And therefore what did that make him and them who promised to love you forever and didn't go through with it? What do you think about them.... temporarily.... when you need this love?

C25 I didn't think of them I just thought of me in terms of they're right, I'm a terrible person.

T26 That's one thing.... (Fiona: I put it all on me).... but now let's get to the anger, did you also at times, not all the time, hate them for not giving you the love that you thought you needed?

C26 Of course I did.

T27 Ah - you see now that's two things. We start with I need the love, I should do the right thing and isn't it terrible, I'm an awful person when I don't, but then they should see my neediness and they should give in to it and they're terrible people if they don't. And then finally, or maybe not even finally, you add to that "now I see I'm angry at the people I love and they love me less and isn't it horrible to be out of control and so brattish and so angry", and you go right back to putting yourself down - isn't that right.... (Fiona: Correct) .... Right.

Now let's just unravel a couple of these things and show you what to do because I think it's very complicated - actually we've done it very, very briefly so you think a lot more about this - but I think it starts with a need to do well and to be loved yourself. Then you get upset, self-downing (when you don't do well and get the love you think you need); then you get angry at them for not giving it; then you get angry at you for being angry at them and maybe losing control, being brattish. But let's just take one of these things again, get back to that - the fundamental need to be loved, to do well with others. Now I'm not going to by any means debate or dispute your desire because everybody desires love. It's one of the most fine, the greatest things in the world, it really makes for relating, but you from the start and right now have to be loved and you need to be loved and you're viewing yourself as a terrible person when you're not. Now why must you be loved, not why do you desire it, why do you have to be....?

[Having identified Fiona's basic problem as a dire need tor love and approval, and her anger as a defence against the 'hurt' to her ego when she doesn't get the love and approval she demands, Ellis invites Fiona to challenge her irrational belief that she needs - not desires - but absolutely needs love.]

C27 It's an interesting point um .... throughout my life it's always been, life was, I never was myself in terms of .... I never knew who I was because I was always going by the standards of what their expectations for me were.

T28 Right or what you thought their expectations were.

C28 Or what I thought their expectations were .... (Ellis: Right) .... and primarily it seemed that I .... er .... I had to be married you know .... (Ellis: Right) .... in a very secure situation ....so that's how I based my life .... not in terms of what was expected of me.

T29 Right. To be a good person I had to fulfil what they expected of me.

C29 So I've never never really done anything for me. I really never found out what I really need.

T30 Well, how can you when you're fundamentally ...

C30 I couldn't and at this time of my life I'm trying to. So what I've done is eliminated love completely from my life, in fact people. I'm totally alone now.

T31 But that throws out the baby with the bath water. Now suppose we could get you to see that you don't need love, it's very desirable, but you don't need it and you don't have to conform to what other people say you should conform to, though it would be nice if they did care for you, and then you would be able to risk getting involved if you really got rid of that dire necessity for doing the right thing and being loved. Now how could that be done? How could any human, you included, get rid of not the desire, we're not trying to get rid of that, 'cos you've really thrown out the baby with the bathwater, the desire .... (Fiona: At this point, yes).... How can you keep the desire to be loved, to be approved, to get along with others, to relate, and not the necessity, the dire need that puts you down. How could you do that?

[Here Ellis puts much emphasis on helping Fiona to keenly discriminate between her dogmatic must and her non-dogmatic preference.]

C31 Well, I think by becoming my own person, number one.

T31 That would be one. That's excellent because then you see you'd risk being you and your philosopy would be: "I'm going to be me at all costs" and .... (Fiona: Right) .... and if they don't love me what could you conclude? They don't love me when I'm me, what could you conclude about that?

C32 Well, it's not that I'm a bad person though .... (Ellis: Right) .... which is something I'm trying to work on.

T33 Right. You could conclude: "maybe it's too bad, I would wish they would like me as me and there must be somebody in the universe who would like me as me, you see, but they don't have to" - it's the necessity, (pounds for emphasis) the demand that does it, not the desire. Now if you could really work on that "I'd like to be me" primarily and then secondarily get those people to care for me who will accept me as ME. Wouldn't that solve a great deal of the problem?

C33 Yes, because I think at that point - if it should ever happen again - um .... it would be a healthy relationship .... (Ellis: Right) .... it would not be that neurotic need and that provocation and that anger.

T34 And you've already implied from what you said a couple of minutes ago - the active solution, because if you would change your philosophy "I'm primarily going to be me and if they like me, great, but if they don't like me I can still accept myself as me", that would be fine if you thought that way, but one way to think that way is what you said "to take risks" and what you might try are some of our shame-attacking exercises. Do you know anything about those?

[At T34 Ellis introduces the idea behind shame-attacking exercises which he describes as voluntary exercises in risk-taking in which clients publicly engage in behaviours normally considered silly or foolish with a view to helping themselves to overcome the anxiety and negative self-rating they may experience when they act poorly in front of others, and especially significant others.]

C34 No, I've no idea.

T35 Well, you think of something that you consider shameful to do in public, in front of people, now not to hurt anybody, we don't want you to slap anybody in the fact or get arrested - walk naked, you could walk naked in a public square and that would be shameful, - but something like not tipping a waiter or a taxi-cab driver .... [Fiona: (laughs): Oh I do that] .... Well that's not it then ....or buy an outlandish costume dress and then never wearing it because you're ashamed to .... (Fiona: Because of the shame) .... Yeah, you see something that you consider shameful. We get people to do foolish things, we get them to go on the New York subway, for example, and to yell out the stops "42nd STREET" at the top of their lungs and to stay on the train, you see. Or to go to Macey's or Bloomingdale's department stores and yell out the time "11.50 AND A THIRD" and to stand there with everybody looking at them. Or to take a banana and a long leash and to walk the banana, and take another banana and feed the first banana - to do foolish things. In public you can go right out onto the street and stop somebody and say "I just got out of the loony-bin, what day is it?"

C35 Well, what purpose will that serve? .... (Ellis: The purpose is that you can pick something) .... that this is what I'm doing and I don't care about the rest of the world?

T36 Well, to pick something that you consider shameful, not that I do, and to do it in public - that's the first part, not get arrested, not get into trouble, and then as you do it in public to work on not feeling ashamed, because shame is the essence of self-downing, of self-hatred, you see, and if you can do these things in public and really not feel ashamed because you know why you're doing them, you know you're doing them for you, you know in this case they're even therapeutic, then that kind of thing helps you to resist the pressure which people have put on you since early childhood - and always will - and stops you from downing yourself.

C36 But why does it have to be something so absurd?

T37 Well, it doesn't. I'm just saying .... actually it would be better if you pick something that you are normally ashamed to do and it would be helpful for you ....

C37 Yeah .... like .... getting angry.

T38 That's right, you could do that ....

C38 Like screaming at someone.

T39 That's right you could deliberately scream. You'd pick somebody that's not too vulnerable - because we don't want you to hurt them - we don't want you to pick a little child or something like that, but somebody that you could get temporarily angry towards - scream at them, because you feel ashamed, then not feel ashamed, and then later show them why you did it, you see, because we don't want anybody else to be hurt in the process. Or something else where you would really be thoroughly ashamed to do it, to risk it because all your life you have avoided this risk, you've sat on your feelings, you've sat on your anger, you've sat on everything and avoided it. Now if we can get you to do it and not put yourself down, not feel ashamed, that would be a long way towards solving your problems. You see? Then you could look at your anger, when you feel angry inside and you feel enraged with people and also acknowledge that you're creating the anger; do you know why you are creating the anger?

C39 Can you repeat that last ....?

T40 When .... let's suppose, ... give me an instance recently where you got angry at somebody, you got very angry .... you just felt it, not that you expressed it.

C40 I don't express it. Um .... someone I work with .... she .... everything goes right for her .... she gets all the great accounts, she gets dates, she gets roses sent to her every day, and I sit there and my stomach is in knots and I feel like saying - and then she complains .... "Oh" .... "Ooh" .... You know she's just a spoilt person who has no true values, she's not sensitive and caring and she .... everything good happens to her and I hate her .... (Ellis: Alright) .... and I get very angry because she hurt me as well.

T41 Right .... so at A, an activating event in the ABCs of REBT, she acts this way and let's suppose she is doing you in and she's acting badly, and she's a spoilt brat herself. Let's assume that .... (Fiona: This is her) .... Exactly .... And at C a consequence in your gut, you're feeling enraged, you're not doing anything about it. No .... but you're feeling enraged. Now in Rational Emotive Behaviour Therapy we think that you are making yourself enraged. She is not enraging you ....

C41 You are right about that .... (Ellis: Right, so what are you doing?) .... no-one else is being annoyed by her ....

T42 That's exactly the point .... (Fiona: Only I:) .... Right so at B your belief system, you are telling yourself something about her that is making you angry and I could guess from our theory, our ABC theory, what it is - but let's see if you could figure it out. What are you saying whenever you are angry at her?

[Here, Ellis tries to get Fiona to work out for herself how she makes herself angry, rather than tell her directly how she creates her own anger.]

C42 Oh I know what I'm saying .... (Ellis: What?) .... She doesn't deserve it, why her? .... (Ellis: Why her?) .... why her? I'm working so much harder and I have had so many more problems in my life, why is everything good happening to her .... (Ellis: As?) .... she doesn't deserve it.

T43 Right and she shouldn't be getting away with this. That's what I hear .... (Fiona: Right). Alright, now we ask in REBT - we go on to D, disputing: why shouldn't (pounds for emphasis) she act that way and get away with it? Why must she act well?

C43 There is no why, there is no reason why she should do anything.

T44 That's right. Now if you really believe that, you believe it at this second, then you would be sorry and displeased and annoyed at her behaviour, but you wouldn't be upset and angry at her. If you really believe that she should act the way she does because she does ....

C44 Not that she should, I mean this is a person, her own personality, and her own whatever .... um .... I can't have her feel or think the way I do .... (Ellis: Right) .... but it does upset me to think she's intelligent enough that she should be able to see it and she doesn't ....

T45 But I say that she shouldn't be able to see it .... (Fiona: I understand that) .... do you know why she shouldn't be able - even though she's intelligent - why should she act the way she does? Do you know why she should?

C45 She shouldn't ....

T46 No, she should.
C46 Oh why she should act the way she is .... (Ellis: Badly) .... because this is her.

T47 That's her nature .... Right .... (Fiona: That's right) .... Now whenever we're angry we're denying the nature of others, I'm assuming with you, it's bad, obnoxious, annoying that she should act annoyingly if that's her nature to act annoyingly.

C47 Just as I should get angry if that's how I feel ....

T48 That's exactly right. Now it's not good that she acts that way nor even that you get angry. You'd better be assertive (pounds for emphasis) without anger, because anger is a damnation of her, you're damning her for her act, and if you're wise you'll say: "Dammit I don't like what she is doing, I wish she wouldn't, and I'll probably tell her one of these days about it and try to get her to change".

[In T46, 47 and 48, Ellis makes the important point that when someone is behaving badly, they should (empirically) be acting badly because they are, and it makes no sense to argue that they shouldn't be doing what they indubitably are doing. He further stresses the important difference between assertively expressing dislike for a person's behaviour and damning that person as a human being for that behaviour.]

C48 Oh I would love to, that would be a very good step in the right direction.

T49 Right, but if we got you un-angry but still displeased with her behaviour and then assertive, and we got you to not down yourself in case she and other people come back (pounds for emphasis) at you when you're assertive, wouldn't that solve the problem?

C49 It would certainly help.

T50 Right, then the thing to do, and you can do it in both orders, you can work on the anger first or the self-downing, the holding yourself in first. I'd advise you to first work on the self-downing, the shame, and determine that hereafter whenever things like this happen with people like her - and she's just an example, there are thousands of them - I will always think my thoughts and accept my thoughts and my feelings about her, and even if she learns about my feelings, because I may tell her, and she puts me down, I will accept myself no matter what she and other people think .... (Fiona: I see) .... You see, I won't say I'm right because I may be wrong, but even when I'm wrong I'll accept myself, because I am I, and I have the right to be wrong. Now I'll try to be correct, but I don't have to be correct, I don't have to be approved by them you see, ...Then secondly, - now that I'm ready to accept myself, I'll see that (1) I am displeased by her behaviour, but (2) I am damning her, I'm saying she must not do what she is indubitably doing and she must do it right now because that's the way she is right now, I wish she wouldn't, and therefore I will assert myself and take the risk she won't love me, she won't like me at all, but she doesn't have to change, it is just highly desirable. D'you see?

C50 Absolutely.

T51 Now if we can get you to work along that line - on mainly self-downing, because I still think that's your biggest problem .... and incidentally we'll go to one other thing and that is: let's suppose now that you are trying to work along the lines we're saying and you still run away, you still don't assert yourself and you don't go for yourself, and you run away and you avoid the situation, you cop out etcetera. Now again at A, activating event, you're copping out, you're not expressing yourself, you're not being yourself. At B, your belief system, you're telling yourself something which we'll get back to in a second, and then at C, you're feeling ashamed of your own copping out, because at B what are you saying again about you for copping out, for not expressing your feelings?

C51 I'm feeling angry .... (Ellis: Right) .... I'm feeling the anger.

T52 Right, but what are you saying about not expressing feelings and copping out and running out of the situation and withdrawing? What are you saying about you, you know you're angry, you know you're non-assertive and you're not doing anything, now what are you telling yourself about your behaviour of copping out?

C52 At that point?

T53 Yeah, when you notice that you've copped out and not said anything.

C53 Well, let's see .... I can't really verbalise it ....

T54 Well, you're not liking yourself are you? .... (Fiona: No, I know that) .... so you're saying, I copped out.

C54 I'm er .... I'm that bad person again. (Ellis: That's right) .... I'm that stupid person, I'm that incompetent person, that child, whatever ....

T55 That's right. Now you see the vicious circle; you began with self-downing to begin with and that's probably why you didn't speak up. You made yourself very angry. Then you were non-assertive about your feelings and on both levels, the original one to down yourself and not speak up, and then you blame yourself for not speaking up, so you do a double whammy .... [Fiona: (laughs): It's a vicious circle, right] .... Right, you see. Now I say that if you start at the end again and say to yourself - "Yes I didn't express myself, that was foolish because I would like her to know, as long as I don't get fired or something, how I feel about her, but if I don't, I don't. If I act poorly that's only a poor act and I'm never a rotten person because I don't have to act well, no matter how desirable it is. Then you'll get rid of downing yourself for your lack of expression of your feelings and then you'll get back and be able to assert yourself and I think even (pounds for emphasis) definitely, determinedly, rather than angrily. When you're not angry at yourself, you'll be able to show her that she's not doing the right thing, but that she's not a total louse for not doing the right thing. Do you see what I mean?

[Here Ellis is adopting a didactic rather than a Socratic approach, actively teaching Fiona the elements of her vicious circle.]

C55 Yes absolutely ....

T56 Now if you would practice that; first just see that you down yourself, your father, her, nobody can down you, you do it by downing yourself, by needing love, and needing to do the right thing. Secondly, seeing that when you're angry and you damn others, you put them down rather than their behaviour; and then thirdly when you see that you are not expressing your feelings, you go right back again to damning yourself. Now do you see that you're the one that is creating your self-downing and that you never have to, you can change that philosophy, then you could really change this. And then you could actively do it by doing our shame-attacking exercises, or, taking other risks to speak up would be one of the main things you could do, because you feel ashamed at times of speaking up. What's shameful about expressing your feelings even if people don't like you? Why is that shameful?

C56 Well, I've never looked at it as shameful. I've looked at it as .... my opinions weren't that .... um how can I put this .... (Ellis: They weren't worthwhile?) .... Yeah, lack of confidence in my own conviction.

T57 But that's another word for shame. If I expressed myself, my feelings and my opinions aren't good enough and that's terrible, that's bad, that's shameful. You see that's just another form of shame.

C57 So shame .... it takes the place of a lot of other expressions .... and feelings.

T58 That's right, self-downing, feelings of inadequacy, self-hatred, lack of confidence, they're all: "I must do well and be loved and isn't it terrible and I'm no good if I'm not." Now if you could see that and think against it and act against it, then you would be doing a very good thing, and that's the homework I'd give you. To see that you're creating especially your shame, that you can change the philosophy that creates it and then you can act shamelessly, but don't get into trouble, just act that way and take risks and see that you never have to down yourself for anything. Now do you think you could work on that?

[Ellis teaches Fiona that shame takes various forms such as, self-downing, feelings of inadequacy, self-hatred and lack of confidence and that they all spring from the same basic irrational belief, "I must do well and be loved, and isn't it terrible, and I'm no good if I'm not."].

C58 I know I could work on it ....

T59 And it will take a while ....

C59 That's the point, it's not going to be a revelation, I know that ....

T60 Right, it's simple, but it's not easy and it takes a while. Now if you do that, then I think you'll feel much better and then be able to take the new philosophy of "I always accept myself no matter what" into other situations. So we're just using this as an illustration .... O.K. it was very nice talking to you, and you just go and think about that and work on that.

C60 I shall. Thank you.

CHAPTER SEVEN

CORRECTING MISCONCEPTIONS ABOUT RATIONAL EMOTIVE BEHAVIOUR THERAPY

Once trainees on initial training courses have acquired some basic information about the theory and practice of REBT, we have found it helpful for the training process to invite questions and reactions from trainees on what they have learned about REBT so far. The type of questions and the reactions that arise at this point often reveal important misunderstandings about the theoretical underpinnings of REBT and how it is practised. Dealing with these misunderstandings is an important part of the training process. If trainees' misunderstandings are left uncorrected at this stage in their training, further misunderstandings will appear later, and trainees will get less benefit from their training than if their doubts and reservations had been addressed at the time they were first brought up. Essentially we attempt to respond to trainee misconceptions about REBT in the same way, and for the same reasons, as we attempt to respond to client misperceptions about the therapy and the ideas upon which its practice is based, i.e. with tact, sensitivity and respect. Most people would agree that when learning a new skill, the earlier one's errors and mis- understandings are identified and corrected, the better it will be for one's future progress. We have compiled the following list of seventeen major misconceptions that trainees have about REBT based on our own experience in training trainees, the experiences of other REBT trainers and the REBT literature (e.g. Dryden, 1995a, 1995b; Dryden & Gordon, 1990; Gandy, 1985; Saltzberg & Elkins, 1980; Young, 1979). These reservations that trainees frequently bring up are presented below in the form of typical questions that trainees ask.

Question 1: REBT states that activating events don't cause emotions. I can see that this is the case when negative events are mild or moderate, but don't very negative events like being raped or losing a loved one cause disturbed emotions?

Answer: Your question directly impinges on the distinction that REBT makes between healthy and unhealthy negative emotions (Dryden, 1990, 1994a, 1995a). Let's take the example of rape that you mentioned. Being raped is undoubtedly a tragic event for both men and women, and as such, it is healthy for the person who has been raped to experience a high degree of distress. According to REBT theory it is healthy to experience an intensely negative event as very distressful because in REBT a keen distinction is made between healthy distress and unhealthy disturbance (Dryden, 1994a). From your earlier studies you may recall that healthy distress stems from a person's rational beliefs about a negative activating event, whilst unhealthy disturbance stems from her irrational beliefs about the same event. Thus, if we look at the typical beliefs that a person has about being raped, we will see that the rational beliefs she holds are an integral part of the rape experience, whereas her irrational beliefs are not. Beliefs that are an integral part of an experience describe real events; they describe what actually happened. In a typical case of rape, for example, they reflect the pain, the fear, the feeling of powerlessness, and of being subjected to an experience of such stark negativity as to overwhelm the person's resources for dealing with it. When a person has been raped, her intense distress stems from her strongly held rational beliefs about this extremely negative A. As virtually everyone who has been subjected to some extremely negative event or stressor such as being hijacked, subjected to torture, or raped will have strongly held rational beliefs about this event, we could almost say that being raped or subjected to intense pain if fear 'causes' intense healthy distress. Of course, strictly speaking, the Stimulus does not cause the Response directly but acts via the Organism to produce the Response. It is the particular biosocial makeup of humans that determines the (human) response. Other living creatures with different biologies would respond differently to the same set of life threatening stressors than would a human (Ellis, 1978).

Examples of rational beliefs an individual would typically have about being raped are:

'It is certainly very bad that this has happened to me.'

'I have been put through a very traumatic experience, made especially traumatic by my inability to prevent it, and I wish to hell it had never happened.'

'My life has hardly been ruined, but I have obviously suffered a severe blow to my sense of myself as an autonomous person in charge of her own life, and I may well suffer still further distress arising from physical and psychological after effects of my distressing experience.'

'Nevertheless, while the quality of my life may not be all that wonderful for a while, and however stressful it may be temporarily, it isn't awful, it isn't the end of the world, but only a darned inconvenience that I'm determined to cope with to the best of my ability.'

Now, a cardinal tenet of REBT is the principle of emotional responsibility. This principle states that people are responsible for their own emotional disturbance because they are responsible for changing their rational beliefs about their negative experiences into irrational beliefs about these experiences. As you know, emotional disturbance stems from, and is maintained by the person's irrational beliefs. People retain this responsibility for their emotionally disturbed feelings even when they encounter tragic adversities such as rape, even though it is very understandable that they do this.

Now, if we look at the irrational beliefs people typically hold about being raped, we see that these beliefs are not an integral part of the rape experience, but rather they are "add-ons" - they consist of exaggerated evaluations and unverifiable conclusions which people bring to their unfortunate experience. Examples of irrational beliefs are:

'I absolutely should have stopped this from happening.'

'This has completely ruined my life.'

'Being raped means that I am a worthless person.'

Whilst it is understandable that people who have undergone a rape experience or some other equally obnoxious experience should think this way, this does not alter the fact that they are still responsible for bringing these irrational beliefs to the experience, and thereby making it seem worse than it already is. It is for this reason that REBT theory holds that very negative A's do not 'cause' emotional disturbance. This is actually an optimistic position, because if very negative events did cause emotional disturbance, then people would be at the mercy of every negative event that happened to them and would have a much harder time overcoming their disturbed feelings than they do now on the assumption that these feelings stem largely from their irrational beliefs.

One more point. Some REBT therapists distinguish between disturbed emotions that are experienced by someone at the time a very negative event happens to them, and disturbed feelings that persist well after the event has occurred. These therapists would argue that being raped does 'cause' disturbed feelings when the event occurs and for a short period afterwards, but if the person's disturbed feelings persist well after the event, then the person who has been raped is responsible for the perpetuation of her disturbance via the creation and perpetuation of her irrational beliefs. These therapists take the position that time-limited irrationalities in response to very negative activating events are not unhealthy reactions, but the perpetuation of these irrationalities is unhealthy. Thus, these REBT therapists argue that a very negative event like rape does 'cause' emotional disturbance in the short term, but not in the long term (for a fuller discussion of time-limited irrationalities see Dryden, 1994b).

Question 2: I'm worried about the principle of emotional responsibility you brought up in response to the previous question. Doesn't it lead to blaming the victim?

Answer: You have raised one of two criticisms that make up the principle of emotional responsibility which is so central to REBT theory, the other being the cop-out criticism. We will deal with each in turn.

In answer to the previous question, we showed that when someone is raped, it is possible to argue that this very negative A 'causes' the intense healthy distress that the person almost invariably experiences. However, if she experiences emotional disturbance, particularly a long time after the event happened, then according to REBT theory she is responsible for her disturbed feelings that are triggered by the irrational beliefs that she brings to the event. However, there is a world of difference between being responsible for one's disturbance and being blamed for having these feelings. In this situation the concept of responsibility means that the person largely disturbs herself about the event because of the irrational beliefs she brings to it. By contrast, the concept of blame here means that someone believes that the person absolutely should not experience such disturbed feelings and is something of a bad person for having these feelings. This is obviously nonsense for two reasons. First, if the person disturbs herself about being raped it is because all the conditions are in place for her to do so. In other words, if she holds a set of irrational beliefs about the event, then empirically she should disturb herself about it. It is obviously inconsistent with reality for someone to demand that the person absolutely should not disturb herself in this way. Second, even if we agree that it is bad for her to disturb herself (and this is a big if) there is no reason or justification to conclude that she is a bad person for disturbing herself. All we can legitimately say is that we have evidence that she is a fallible human being who understandably holds a set of irrational beliefs about a tragic event. Rather than being blamed for her disturbance, she should preferably be helped to overcome it. Ironically, some people would blame her if she wasn't emotionally upset about being raped. These people would say she ought to feel ashamed of herself, and if she isn't, that shows she is just a 'shameless hussy' with no self respect!

A close ally of this idea that a person should be blamed for being raped, is the belief held by some people that she is responsible for being raped and therefore should be blamed for it happening. This again is nonsense. Let us be quite clear about this. Rape inevitably involves coercion. Even if the woman is responsible for 'leading the man on' - an expression popular with defence counsels in courtroom rape trials - he is responsible for raping her. Nothing, including whether the woman experiences distressing or disturbed feelings, absolves him from this responsibility. So, if a woman has been raped nothing that she did or failed to do detracts from the fact that the rapist is solely responsible for committing the rape. As such, the woman cannot be held responsible for being raped. She can be held responsible for 'leading the man on' if this can be shown to be the case, but she cannot, repeat cannot, be held responsible for being raped.

In short, the principle of emotional responsibility means in this situation that the woman is responsible for her disturbed feelings only. She is not to be blamed for this, nor is she to be held responsible for being raped no matter how she behaved in the situation.

Let us now deal with the cop-out criticism sometimes levelled against the principle of emotional responsibility. The cop-out criticism can be stated thus. If a person is largely responsible for her own disturbed feelings, then if you act nastily towards her and she upsets herself about your behaviour, all you have to say is that because she largely disturbs herself about your bad behaviour then her feelings have nothing to do with you. Thus you give yourself carte blanche to say or do anything you wish on the grounds that if a person upsets herself about your bad behaviour, that is her lookout, not yours.

Earlier on in this answer, we pointed out that a rapist is responsible for carrying out a rape regardless of how the person who has been raped feels and regardless of any so-called mitigating circumstances. Now if I act nastily towards you I am responsible for my behaviour regardless of how you feel about my behaviour. If my behaviour is nasty then I cannot be absolved of responsibility for my action just because you are largely responsible for your making yourself disturbed about my nasty behaviour. Don't forget, if my behaviour is that bad, it is healthy for you to hold strongly a set of rational beliefs about it and, whereas I cannot be held responsible for your disturbance, I can be said to be responsible for your distress. Thus, I cannot 'cop-out' of my responsibility for my own behaviour nor for 'distressing' you.

The cop-out criticism is also made of the REBT position on guilt. As I (WD) have shown in my book, Overcoming Guilt (Dryden, 1994c), guilt is an unhealthy emotion that stems from a set of irrational self-blaming beliefs about breaking one's moral code, for example. The healthy alternative to guilt is remorse which stems from a set of rational self-accepting beliefs about a moral code violation. The important point to note about remorse is that it does not absolve the person from taking responsibility for breaking his or her moral code. It does not, in short, encourage the person to 'cop-out' of assuming responsibility for what he did. Apparently this is a difficult point for some people to grasp.

For example, Marjorie Proops, a famous agony aunt, claimed to have read the above book on guilt - in which I (WD) continually reiterate the non 'cop-out' position of remorse - but said in response to a letter from a reader who sought help to stop feeling guilty about sleeping with her best friend's husband that the reader SHOULD feel guilty. Proops feared that remorse and even guilt (which she clearly failed to differentiate) would provide the person with a 'cop-out' or an excuse for continuing to act immorally. The truth is, however, very different. Remorse is based on the rational belief, 'I wish I hadn't broken my moral code, but there is no reason why I absolutely should not have broken it. I broke it because of what I was telling myself at the time. Now let me accept myself and think how I can learn from my past behaviour so that I can act morally in future.' As you see, in remorse the person takes responsibility for her behaviour, is motivated to act better next time by her rational belief which also enables her to learn from her moral code violation. By contrast, guilt is based on an irrational belief which will either encourage her to deny responsibility for her past action or interfere with her attempt to learn from it. So far from encouraging the person to 'cop-out' of her responsibility, the principle of emotional responsibility encourages the person to take responsibility for her actions and for her disturbed guilt feelings. It further encourages the person to challenge her irrational, guilt-producing beliefs and adopt a rational, remorse-invoking philosophy so that she can learn from her past behaviour, make appropriate amends and take responsibility for her future behaviour.

Question 3: You have discussed the ABCs of REBT, but I find this overly simplistic. Isn't the theory of REBT too simple?

Answer: First, in answer to your question we have presented enough of the theory of REBT to help get you started with its practice. Don't forget that you are on a first-level training course on REBT. If we presented the full complexity of the ABCs of REBT, then we would run the risk of overwhelming you with too much information too soon. In reality, as Albert Ellis (1991) has recently shown and as I (WD) have myself demonstrated (Dryden, 1994a) the ABCs interact in often complex ways. Let us give you a few examples of this complexity. So far, as you have rightly observed, we have introduced the simple version of the ABCs where A occurs first, and is then evaluated at B to produce an emotional and/or behavioral consequence at C. This is the version of the ABCs that is usually taught on first-level training courses and that we, as practitioners, teach our clients.

Now let us introduce some complexity into the picture. If a person holds an irrational belief about an event, then he will tend to create further distorted inferences about this A. For example, if you believe that you must be loved by your partner (iB) and he shouts at you (A1) then you will be more likely to think that he doesn't love you and is thinking of leaving you (A2) than if you have an alternative rational belief (rB). So, instead of the usual formula: $A > B > C$, we have $A1 > iB > A2$.

Second, if a person is already experiencing an unhealthy negative emotion then this will lead him to attend to certain aspects in a situation. Thus, if you are already anxious, then you are more likely to focus on threatening aspects of a situation than if you are concerned, but not anxious. Putting this into a formula, we have $C > A$.

We hope these two examples have given you a flavour of the complexities of the ABCs of REBT and have helped you to see that whilst in its rudimentary form the ABC model is simple, its full version is neither too simple nor simplistic.

Question 4: I get the impression that REBT neglects the past. Am I right?

Answer: As we have shown, REBT states that people disturb themselves (C) by the beliefs (B) that they hold about the negative activating events in their lives (A). Now A's can be present events, future events and past evens. Thus if a client is disturbed now about certain aspects of her past, then an REBT therapist would certainly deal with this using the ABC framework where A is the past event (or · events).

What REBT questions, however, is the idea that the client's past MADE him disturbed now in the present. This, you will recall, is an example of 'A causes C' thinking to which REBT objects. Now, even if we assume temporarily that the client was made disturbed as a child by a past event, or more usually by an ongoing series of events, REBT theory argues that the reason that the person is disturbed now about his past is because in the present he holds a set of irrational beliefs that he has actively kept alive or perpetuated from the past. Actually, the situation is more complex than this because REBT holds that we are not, as children made disturbed by events; rather, we bring our tendencies to disturb ourselves to these events. Thus, REBT adheres to a constructivist position even about the origins of psychological disturbance.

We have stressed that the REBT therapist certainly works with the past mainly by looking at the client's presently-held irrational beliefs about his past. In addition, the therapist can consider the client's past disturbed feelings about specific or ongoing historical situations and help him to see what irrational beliefs he was holding then to create those disturbed feelings. We have also found it useful to make the past present by, for example, encouraging the client to have a two-chair dialogue with figures from the past for the purpose of identifying, challenging and changing the client's present irrational beliefs about these figures. This technique has to be used sensitively as it often provokes strong affect.

To summarise, REBT does not ignore a client's past, but works with past material either by disputing currently held irrational beliefs about historical events or by challenging the past irrational beliefs that the client may have held about these same events. However, REBT guards against A > C thinking by making it clear that it does not think that past events cause present disturbance.

Question 5:   Doesn't the REBT concept of acceptance encourage complacency?

Answer: The REBT concept of acceptance certainly gives rise to a lot of confusion in many people's minds.   Some, like you, consider that it leads to complacency, others think it means indifference; yet others judge it to mean that we should condone negative events.   Actually it means none of these things.   Let us carefully spell out what REBT theory does mean by the term 'acceptance'.

The first point we wish to stress is that acceptance means acknowledging the existence of an event, for example, and that all the conditions were in place for that event to occur. However, it does not mean that it is necessarily good that the event happened, nor that there is nothing one can do to rectify the situation. Let's suppose that I betray your trust. By accepting this event, you would acknowledge that I did in fact betray you, that unfortunately all the conditions were in place for this betrayal to occur, namely that I had a set of thoughts which led me to act in the way that I did. Accepting my betrayal also means that whilst you actively, strongly dislike my betrayal (i.e. you certainly don't condone the way I treated you), you do not condemn me as a person for my betrayal. Furthermore, acceptance certainly does not preclude you from taking constructive action to rectify the situation. Acceptance, in short, is based on a set of rational beliefs that leads you to feel healthily negative about my behaviour, rather than emotionally disturbed about what I did.

The same argument applies to the concept of self-acceptance. When I accept myself for breaking my moral code, I regard myself as a fallible human being for my wrongdoing. I do not condone my behaviour; rather, I take responsibility for it, truly strive to understand why I acted in the way that I did, learn from the experience, make appropriate amends and resolve to apply what I have learned from the experience so that, in similar circumstances, I can act morally (Ellis, 1988).

So rather than encouraging complacency, acceptance - when correctly understood - can become the springboard for constructive change.

Question 6: Doesn't REBT tend to neglect clients' emotions?

Answer: The short answer to your question is no. In fact, the opposite is the case. REBT therapists are essentially and fundamentally concerned with clients' emotions; indeed, the whole aim of the therapy is to help clients overcome their emotional problems and by identifying and uprooting their irrational beliefs underlying their problems, to help them experience healthy emotions in response to negative life events, and to lead less frustrating and happier lives. As you will have seen in our answer to Question 1, REBT keenly differentiates between healthy and unhealthy negative emotions about very negative events. Moreover, REBT holds that there are virtually no legitimate reasons why we need make ourselves emotionally disturbed about anything, but allows us full leeway to experience strong healthy negative emotions such as sorrow, regret, displeasure and annoyance. REBT also maintains that when we experience certain self-defeating and unhealthy emotions (such as guilt, depression, anxiety, worthlessness or rage), we are adding an unverifiable element to our rational view that some things in the world are bad and had better be changed. So long as we cling to these unhealthy negative emotions, our ability to change unpleasant conditions (negative A's) will be hindered, rather than helped. The essence of REBT is that emotions are valuable - they stir and motivate us to action, but we had better favour healthy constructive, rather than unhealthy destructive emotions if we wish to survive happily in this world. It is a hallmark of REBT that humans have enormous, though not perfect control over their unhealthy negative emotions if they choose to work at eradicating the bigoted and irrational notions which they employ to create them.

However, REBT therapists do not believe that emotional catharsis is therapeutic per se nor do they encourage their clients to explore the subtle nuances of their emotions. Rather, they encourage their clients to acknowledge their feelings, to feel their feelings, but thence to detect and dispute the irrational beliefs that underlie their unhealthy negative feelings and to replace them with healthy, constructive alternatives. So whereas REBT therapists certainly do not neglect their client's emotions, neither do they deify them, but they do adopt a particular stance towards emotions as outlined above.

Question 7: My previous counsellor training taught me that the most important ingredient in counselling is the relationship between client and counsellor. Doesn't REBT neglect the therapeutic relationship?

Answer: Carl Rogers (1957) wrote a seminal paper in which he argued that there were a set of necessary and sufficient core conditions that the therapist had to provide and the client had to perceive the therapist as having provided for therapeutic change to occur. Two years later Ellis (1959) published a reply in which he acknowledged that these conditions were important and frequently desirable, but they were hardly necessary and sufficient. This has been the REBT position ever since. Therapists agree that rapport between therapist and client is helpful for ensuring effective treatment. However, in REBT rapport is not deemed helpful or curative in, by, and of itself. Clients do not get better simply because of their good relationship with you. Rapport is helpful because, once it is established, clients are more likely to share their thoughts and feelings honestly with you. This helps you to achieve a valid and quick assessment of their problems. Also, rapport between you and your clients makes them more receptive to your efforts to educate and change their dysfunctional cognitions and behaviours (Ellis, Sichel, Yeager, DiMattia, & DiGiuseppe, 1989).

Thus REBT therapists do not neglect the therapeutic relationship. However, they do not regard the relationship as the sine qua non of therapeutic change. Moreover, as DiGiuseppe et al (1993) discovered, REBT therapists scored as highly as therapists from other schools on measures of the 'core conditions' provided by clients. If we are neglecting the therapeutic relationship, our clients don't seem to think so!

Question 8: REBT therapists may not neglect the therapeutic relationship with their clients, but isn't this relationship unequal?

Answer: It depends on what you mean by unequal. REBT therapists consider themselves to be equal to their clients as humans. The therapist is not more worthy than the client, nor vice versa. However, on different aspects of themselves there are likely to be inequalities. The client may know more about gardening, or motoring, or bridge, or be more sociable than the therapist, for example. They are equal in their humanity, but unequal in certain areas.

Now the purpose of therapy is to help the client to overcome his psychological problems and live more happily, more resourcefully. In this area the therapist claims to know more about the dynamics of emotional problems and facilitating personal change than the client, at least from an REBT perspective, and this does constitute an inequality as do the ones mentioned earlier that are in the client's favour. REBT therapists openly acknowledge this real inequality, but stress that it needs to be placed in the context of a relationship between two equally fallible human beings.

Question 9: How do you respond to the criticism that REBT therapists brainwash their clients?

Answer: First, let's be clear about what we mean by brainwashing. Brainwashing is a process where the person to be brainwashed is isolated from her normal environment and from people whom she knows, is deprived of food, water and sleep and when judged to be in a susceptible state is provided with information and beliefs which are usually counter to the information and beliefs she would normally hold. Obviously, by this definition REBT therapists do not brainwash their clients.

However, we think you mean something more subtle than this. Perhaps you think that REBT therapists tell their clients what to think without due regard for their current views and press them hard to believe the REBT 'line'. If this is what you mean then we would deny that well-trained, ethical REBT therapists would do this (we cannot speak for untrained individuals who pass themselves off as REBT practitioners).

As Dryden (1994d) has pointed out, REBT holds that one of the hallmarks of mental health is the ability to think for oneself and to be sceptical of new ideas, at least initially. In fact, it isn't a bad idea to be sceptical of any idea, new or old, until one is convinced otherwise. REBT regards gullibility, suggestibility and the uncritical acceptance of promulgated ideas as breeding grounds of emotional disturbance. Thus, REBT therapists encourage their clients to think for themselves rather than telling them what to think. REBT therapists adopt the Socratic method of challenging the core irrational philosophies their clients hold about themselves, other people, and the world that underlie their emotional problems. We encourage clients to question their irrational beliefs for their own benefit, not for the therapist's benefit. REBT therapists try to teach their clients the scientific method of logically examining their beliefs, to look for evidence in support of them, and to learn the different between beliefs that are realistic and beliefs that are unrealistic, illogical and irrational. They try to show their clients how thoughts, emotions and behaviour are all interrelated, and that the consequences of rigidly holding dogmatic, irrational, unsustainable beliefs are disturbed emotions and dysfunctional behaviours. Instead of unequivocally telling their clients that some of their beliefs about themselves, other people or the world are inconsistent with reality and self-defeating, REBT therapists try to teach their clients, through Socratic dialogue, how to apply the methods of science to their beliefs and see for themselves that some stoutly held beliefs are simply not viable, and therefore are largely unproductive or self-defeating in the long term.

It is important to note that in presenting rational principles, skilled REBT therapists elicit both their client's understanding of these concepts and their views of these ideas. There usually follows a healthy debate between client and therapist where the therapist aims to correct the client's misconceptions of these rational principles in a respectful manner (as we hope we are demonstrating with you now). At no time does the therapist insist that the client must believe the rational concepts he is being taught. If the therapist were to do so, this would be evidence of therapist irrationality: 'I have to get my clients to think rationally and if I fail in this respect that proves that I am a lousy therapist and a less worthy person as a result.'

You will recall that we stressed that REBT therapists encourage their clients to voice their doubts and reservations about REBT and take these seriously. This is also the antithesis of brainwashing. While it is true that REBT therapists have a definitive viewpoint concerning the nature of psychological disturbance and which conditions facilitate therapeutic change (as do virtually all therapists of whatever persuasion), it is also true that REBT therapists are open with their clients concerning these views and strive to present them as clearly as they can. However, as we stated earlier, just because REBT therapists teach REBT principles to their clients, it does not follow that they are attempting to brainwash their clients or impose their views upon them.

As I (WD) make clear, my own practice is to explain to my clients that (a) I will be offering them a specific approach to therapy based on a particular framework; (b) that there are other approaches to therapy that offer different frameworks; and (c) that I am happy to make a referral if it transpires that the client is better served by a different therapeutic approach. I believe that many REBT therapists act similarly with their clients. This, I hope you will agree, is a long way from brainwashing. REBT therapists have preferred therapeutic goals, but are prepared to make compromises if it becomes clear that the client is unwilling or unable to work towards the therapeutic goal of philosophic change. I have yet to hear of a brainwasher who is prepared to make compromises! (Dryden, 1995a).

Question 10: But don't REBT therapists tell their clients what to feel and what to do?

Answer: As we stated in our answer to Question 9, REBT therapists keenly discriminate between healthy and unhealthy negative emotions. We assume that clients come to therapy in the first instance because they are not achieving their basic goals and because they have developed habitual dysfunctional patterns which keep getting them into trouble. For example, clients may repeatedly respond to negative events in their lives by over-reacting or under-reacting emotionally, and may be quite unaware that their psychological problems arise from their misperceptions and irrational beliefs about what they perceive is happening to them. Even when they know that they are behaving poorly, clients will keep repeating non-adjustive or unhealthy emotional responses to negative environmental situations. REBT therapists' initial goal therefore is to help clients minimise their disturbance about their negative A's, while encouraging them to acknowledge, experience and channel their healthy distress about these A's. However, REBT therapists make clear that their clients have a choice concerning their feelings and behaviour. Just because REBT theory advocates that clients minimise their unhealthy disturbed feelings, but not their healthy distressed feelings, it does not follow that clients have to agree with this view. The same is true of the client's behaviour. An REBT therapist may well point out to her client the self-defeating nature of his present behaviour, but she does not insist that the client follow her lead. As with the issue of beliefs, REBT therapists have preferences concerning how clients feel and behave in relation to the issue of psychological health and disturbance and they may well articulate these preferences during therapy. After all, they genuinely want to help their clients live psychologically healthy lives and they believe they have a good theory to help their clients do this. However, REBT therapists firmly respect their client's freedom and do not transmute their preferences into musts on this issue, even if this means that a particular client may continue to perpetuate her psychological problems. Her REBT therapist will, of course, explore the reasons for this, but will not in the final analysis insist that the client adopt the healthy alternative.

It is worth noting that in areas not related to the issue of psychological health and disturbance, REBT therapists adopt a laissez-faire attitude towards their clients' feelings and behaviour. For example, whether a client pursues stamp-collecting, train-spotting or body building is not the therapist's concern assuming that all these activities are based on the client's preferences and are not harmful to others or to the environment.

Question 11: From what you have been saying, it seems to me that REBT therapists prevent clients from finding their own solutions to their problems. Am I right about this?

Answer: In answering this question, we need to distinguish between two types of solutions: practical solutions and psychological solutions. In REBT a psychological solution to the client's problems mainly involves the client in identifying, challenging and changing his irrational beliefs. Whereas a practical solution involves, amongst other things, the client in responding behaviourally to negative A's in ways which are functional and self-helping. In this analysis, achieving a psychological solution makes it easier for the client to apply the practical solution and, therefore, preferably should be achieved first.

Now, the REBT therapist assumes that the client will not achieve a philosophically-based psychological change on his own. The therapist further assumes that she needs to help the client in active ways to understand what this psychological solution involves and how he can apply it to resolve his problem. Once she has helped the client to do this then the client is generally able to choose what he considers to be the best practical solution to his problem. If the client is unable to choose the best practical solution to his problem, the REBT therapist helps him to specify different practical solutions to his problem, encourages him to list the advantages and disadvantages of each course of action and to select and implement what appears to be the best practical solution.

To summarise, REBT therapists actively encourage their clients to understand and implement REBT-oriented psychological solutions to their emotional problems first before tackling their practical problems. REBT therapists assume that once this is accomplished then clients will often be able to see for themselves which practical solutions make the best sense and implement them. When the therapist does intervene in the practical problem-solving phase of therapy, it is to help the client weigh up the pros and cons of his own generated solutions and to select the most effective course of action.

Question 12: Isn't REBT too confrontational?

Answer: REBT is basically an active-directive approach where the therapist intervenes actively and directs the client to the attitudinal core of his problems and helps him to develop a plan to challenge his self-defeating beliefs that constitute this core. In disputing the client's irrational beliefs, the therapist does take the lead in questioning the client concerning the empirical, logical and pragmatic nature of these beliefs. The disputing techniques of the therapist often seem overly confrontational to therapists who advocate less directive counselling methods. It is the contrast between these methods and the active-directive methods of REBT that lead these therapists to conclude that REBT is TOO confrontational.

If the REBT therapist prepares the client adequately for her active-directive methods, particularly her challenging, disputing techniques, then in general the client will not consider the therapist to be TOO confrontational, although the observing less directive therapist who does not fully understand what the REBT therapist is trying to do might consider this therapist to be overly confrontational. However, if the REBT therapist fails to give a satisfactory rationale for her challenging behaviour then she may well be experienced by her client as TOO confrontational.

Question 13: You say that REBT is a structured therapy, but doesn't it 'straitjacket' clients?

Answer: This is often a criticism levelled against REBT by therapists who prefer to give their clients a lot of 'space' to explore themselves and their concerns. Whilst it is true that REBT is a structured approach to psychotherapy, it is also the case that skilled REBT therapists vary the amount of structure according to what is happening in the session. Thus, at times an REBT therapist may be quite unstructured, for example when her client has started to talk about a newly discovered problem or she may use session structure rather loosely, for example in the ending phase when prompting the client to assess a problem using the ABC framework with little or no coaching from the therapist. Of course, there are other times when the REBT therapist will be quite structured in the way she controls the session, particularly when disputing her client's irrational beliefs. Again, if the therapist provides a rationale for the use of a tight structure and the client understands and assents to this, then the client won't consider that he has been 'straitjacketed' by the therapist although the observer might make such a conclusion.

Question 14: Isn't it the case that REBT is only concerned with changing beliefs?

Answer: While it is undeniably true that changing clients' irrational beliefs is a distinctive feature of REBT theory and a ley element of REBT practice, it is by no means the only or exclusive concern of REBT practitioners. REBT therapists are primarily concerned with helping clients to pursue their basic goals and purposes. To this end, REBT therapists are also concerned with helping clients to change the negative events in their lives where practicable so that they gain more positive outcomes. Changing the negative A's is best done, as argued above, by first changing the irrational beliefs clients may hold about these A's, and replacing them with more rational convictions. While REBT therapists view this as a central goal of therapy, it is not their sole goal. In pursuit of their overall goal of helping clients to pursue their basic goals and purposes, REBT therapists are interested in helping clients to change not only their irrational beliefs and dysfunctional feelings and behaviours, but also their images, their interpersonal relationships and, of course, the aversive events in their lives wherever possible. As such, REBT is a multimodal rather than a unimodal approach to therapy.

An issue similar to the question you raised here relates to how REBT is often portrayed in therapeutic outcome studies. In these studies REBT is deemed to be synonymous with just its cognitive restructuring methods rather than a multimodal approach which also employs emotive, behavioural, imaginal and relationship-enhancing techniques. As such, psychotherapy researchers have also wrongly concluded that REBT therapists are ONLY interested in helping their clients to change the latter's beliefs.

Question 15: REBT relies heavily on verbal interchange between therapist and client. It also advocates concepts that are difficult to grasp. Doesn't this mean that REBT only works with highly verbal, intelligent clients?

Answer: This is a common criticism of REBT and we can understand why you have made it. We have presented REBT to you in its complex sophisticated form. We have used a lot of words and explained its concepts in a way that reflects this complexity. After all, everyone here in this training group is highly verbal and intelligent; otherwise we wouldn't have let you onto the course .... (general laughter). However, while it is true that REBT seems to go down well with people who are bright and have a fair degree of verbal fluency, skilled REBT therapists can also tailor the was they explain REBT concepts to match the verbal and intellectual capacities of their clients. Because this issue is beyond the scope of this book we refer you, in particular, to the work of Knaus & Haberstroh (1993) and Howard Young (see Dryden, 1989) who have written about the application of REBT to clients who are neither particularly verbal nor intelligent.

Question 16: REBT is noted for its concern with rationality. How is a criterion of rationality determined?

Answer: This raises the question of who or what decides whether or not the client is being irrational. Some people would contend that the client is not irrational or disturbed, because given the social environment he lives in, for example, he should be anxious or enraged or otherwise disturbed. We would agree that definitions of rationality and irrationality are somewhat arbitrary - in any of the main systems of psychotherapy, not just in REBT. However, a client usually comes to therapy because he thinks he is getting poor results in living and presumably wants to change his self-defeating ways and become more self confident and secure. Since the client wants to change his ways and become less disturbed and more rational, this is what the REBT therapist will presumably help him to do.

REBT contends that once certain goals, such as being unanxious or unconditionally self-accepting are (by somewhat arbitrary definition) assumed to be "good" and "rational", then a scientifically validatable method of reaching these goals can be established and taught to clients. Thus, the REBT therapist is saying that if emotional disturbance is largely determined by irrational thinking (which in turn leads to over-anxiety, excessive hostility and various other symptoms of dysfunctional behaviour which render the client ineffective and block him from attaining his goals), we can help him change his thinking in a relatively short time by teaching him certain special techniques within a specific theoretical framework to challenge his uncritically held assumptions about himself and the world, by doing certain homework assignments, and by working steadily to desensitize and decondition himself in various specific ways.

However, the assumption that emotional disturbance stems from irrational beliefs is merely a hypothesis, but one which has a good deal of clinical and some empirical support (Ellis & Whiteley, 1979). Further research to empirically validate this assumption would be highly desirable.

Question 17: It has been said that REBT encourages clients to become unfeeling robots. What is your response?

Answer: Nothing could be further from the truth! Indeed, REBT is one of the few therapies which helps clients to discriminate between their unhealthy, self-defeating negative emotions and their healthy, constructive emotions. When clients are faced with negative life events, such as the loss of loved ones, REBT encourages such clients to keenly feel healthy emotions such as sorrow, sadness and grief. An emotion-free existence, even if it could be achieved, has no place in the REBT view of things. Such an existence would seem a very dull, sterile sort of state in which to "live" and could only be achieved by the abandonment of all desires and the creation of an attitude of indifference to the world. That would be the exact opposite of the REBT philosophy, and no real REBT therapist would ever attempt to do any such thing.

We hope that we have dealt satisfactorily and respectfully with the seventeen most common misconceptions of REBT.

CHAPTER EIGHT

PERSONALITY CHARACTERISTICS OF EFFECTIVE REBT THERAPISTS

In my (WD) book with Albert Ellis The Practice of Rational Emotive Behavior Therapy (Ellis & Dryden, 1997), we outline personal qualities of effective Rational Emotive Behaviour Therapists what we have observed in our colleagues - and in those trainees who seem to do well in practising REBT. The more important of these qualities are listed below.

(1) Since REBT is a fairly structured form of therapy, its effective practitioners are usually comfortable with structure, but flexible enough to work in a less structured manner when the need arises.

(2) REBT practitioners tend to be intellectually, cognitively, or philosophically inclined and become attracted to REBT because the approach provides them with opportunities to fully express this tendency.

(3) Since it is advocated that REBT is often conducted in a strong, active-directive manner (Ellis, 1979), effective REBT practitioners are usually comfortable operating in this mode, and are often skilled teachers and communicators. Nevertheless, they have the flexibility to modify their interpersonal style with clients so that they provide the optimum conditions to facilitate client change. For example, REBT therapists often have a good sense of humour and use it appropriately in therapy, but not with all clients.

(4) REBT emphasises that it is important for clients to put their therapy-derived insights into practice in their everyday lives. Consequently, effective practitioners of REBT are usually comfortable with using behavioural methods to facilitate client change, and with providing the active encouragement that clients often require if they are to follow through on homework assignments.

(5) Effective REBT therapists tend to have little fear of failure themselves; this is because they do not invest their personal worth in bringing about their client's improvement; and because they do not need their clients' love/or approval. As such, and as noted later, they are not afraid of taking calculated risks if therapeutic impasses occur.

(6) Effective REBT therapists tend to unconditionally accept both themselves and their clients as fallible human beings and are therefore tolerant of their own errors and the sometimes irresponsible acts of their clients. Effective REBT therapists note their own errors and try to avoid making them in future with other clients, but do not condemn themselves for being error-prone. Practitioners of REBT tend to have, or work persistently towards acquiring, a high level of frustration tolerance. This serves as a good model for clients to emulate and helps therapists to avoid feeling discouraged when their clients improve at a slower rate than desired.

(7) Effective REBT practitioners tend to score highly on the following criteria of positive mental health and as such, serve as healthy role models for their clients.

(a) They practice enlighted self-interest in that they tend to be first and primarily interested in themselves and to put their own interest at least a little above the interests of others. However, they sacrifice themselves to some degree for those for whom they care but not overwhelmingly or completely.

(b) They also have a large measure of social interest, and they realise that if they do not act morally to protect the rights and abet social survival, it is unlikely that they will be helping to create the kind of world in which they themselves can live comfortably and happily.

(c) They are self-directed and assume personal responsibility for their lives while simultaneously preferring to cooperate with others. In doing so, they do not need the support or help of others although they regard these as being desirable.

(d) They are flexible in their thinking and are open to change. That is to say, they do not make rigid and absolutistic rules for themselves or others.

(e) They tend to have a high acceptance of uncertainty and do not demand that they must know what is going to happen to them or to others.

(f) They have a strong commitment to creative pursuits and they realise that they (and others) tend to be healthier and happier when they are virtually absorbed in something outside of themselves.

(g) They are successful in the application of scientific thinking to their own lives and in the practice of therapy. Such therapists tend to regulate their emotions and actions by reflecting on them and evaluating their consequences in terms of the extent to which they lead to the attainment of their short-term and long-term goals. Thus, effective REBT therapists do not tend to be deeply religious, mystically minded or anti-intellectual in outlook.

(h) As noted above, effective REBT therapists accept themselves as fallible human beings and can undefensively acknowledge making errors both within and outside of therapy. In unconditionally accepting themselves, they are less likely to continue making such errors than they would if they denigrated themselves for these errors. REBT therapists accept themselves, note their errors, and patiently try to eliminate these errors or, at least, reduce the frequency of their incidence.

(i) They tend to take a fair number of risks and to try to do what they want to do even where there's a good chance that they might fail. They tend to be adventurous but not foolhardy.

(j) They tend to operate on the principle of long-range hedonism and are willing to forgo short-term pleasures when these interfere with the pursuit of their long-term constructive goals. In this manner, too, they also serve as good role models for clients in that they demonstrate that instant gratification of desires may be counter-productive and may often frustrate the attainment of more important long term goals. In addition, REBT therapists set an example of high frustration tolerance by showing that they do not have to get what they want immediately and can unrebelliously buckle down to doing necessary but boring tasks when it is in their best interests to do so promptly.

(k) They are non-Utopian in outlook and accept the fact that Utopias are probably unachievable. They also accept that it is unlikely that they will get everything they want and that they will frequently experience frustration in their lives.

(l) They accept full responsibility for their own emotional disturbances and will strive to overcome their own emotional and behavioural problems by utilising the methods and techniques of REBT. In the final chapter of this book we will show how we have used the principles and methods of REBT to overcome some of our own psychological problems.

(m) Since REBT advocates the use of techniques in a number of different therapeutic modalities (cognitive, imagery, emotive, behavioural and interpersonal) its effective practitioners are comfortable with a multi-modal approach to treatment and tend not to be people who like to stick rigidly to any one modality.

CHAPTER NINE

TEACHING REBT

Teaching REBT is a rewarding experience for the authors as students are able to discover a therapeutic approach that is relatively short-term in its counselling phase, fundamental in its emotional problem-solving focus and enduring in its impact. Some students, initially, express sheer incredulity that a therapy can often deliver so much in so short a space of time but after using REBT on themselves and/or their clients incredulity is replaced by grudging acceptance or downright amazement. Of course, some students say this approach 'is not for me' as it does not suit their personality style or others shrink from what they perceive to be REBT's attacking, confrontational stance with clients. Chapter seven has examined some of the major misconceptions about REBT. This chapter will discuss some of the main complaints or problems that students present to the REBT trainer/supervisor.

'IT'S ALL SO STRUCTURED'

This usually refers to the 13 step treatment sequence (see chapter five) and the agenda setting of each session which some students liken to doing therapy in a straitjacket - it greatly restricts their freedom to address the clients' presenting problems in a way that is familiar to and comfortable for them. For therapists who have learned non-directive counselling approaches such a highly structured approach can appear anti-therapeutic as clients seem to be led by the nose to the foregone conclusion of the causes of and solutions to their emotional problems, i.e. disputing the disturbance-producing properties of their 'must' and 'should' statements; instead, they believe clients should be allowed to develop competence as their own guide in discovering idiosyncratic remedies to their problems.

Far from being a disadvantage, REBT views its highly structured approach as being both rapid and efficient in cutting a clear pathway through the thickets of the clients' presenting problem. The ABCDE model of emotional disturbance and change (the abbreviated and alphabetical version of the 13 step sequence) provides clients with a lifelong problem-solving tool. In order for clients to learn this model, it is important for them to follow the therapist's lead and not the other way round:

Student: I don't feel that REBT gives me enough latitude to explore the client's problems in a way that I'm used to. I feel hemmed in by all these steps, the structure of the therapy hour and pressed by you to hurry things along.

Trainer: Well, REBT does favour an early problem-solving focus and this won't be achieved if you allow clients to talk interminably or therapy to wander in all directions. It's important to socialize them into REBT at the outset. In this way, they are more likely to gain greater therapeutic benefits because they understand what is expected of them.

Student: It just seems that REBT is a checklist of things to do; as if you're trying to find out what's wrong with a car. I'm not a car mechanic, I'm a therapist. And anyway, it's only a question of time before you get to the client's 'must' and 'should' - no wonder you want to get on with it because you know exactly where you're going.

Trainer: We are a kind of mental health mechanic trying to locate the source of that clanking noise in the client's head. Therefore having a checklist, as you call it, is no bad thing as it keeps both the therapist and client on track. Discard that checklist and the structure of therapy could quickly sag or even disappear. The ABCDE format of REBT is the heart of this approach and therefore has to be taught in a systematic fashion, not in a piecemeal or desultory way. As for your last point, REBTers make no bones about having what they believe is a very good model for understanding and tackling emotional disturbance. Therefore we stick with it.

Student: Yeah, I suppose so. It's just such a radical departure from everything I've learned before. I still can't shake off the idea how prescriptive this approach seems.

Trainer: Well I don't want you to shake it off but to remain open-minded while you are gaining more knowledge and experience of REBT. I hope you will be pleasantly and genuinely surprised how quickly REBTers can help clients to uncover and overcome their underlying problems if they follow the counselling sequence steps.

Student: It's like those footsteps painted on the floor at dancing schools to help you learn the waltz or whatever.

Trainer: Rational emotive ballroom therapy. I like it! But will it help to focus your mind on what you are supposed to be learning?

Student: It might do. I'll give it a whirl.

The 13 steps are not a rigid protocol otherwise they would be dubbed 'Commandments' and not steps. Once REBTers have become proficient in their use and internalised the principles underpinning them, then they can be modified to suit the individual therapist's method of teaching REBT and the clinical population he/she serves.

'I'LL NEVER GET THE HANG OF THIS'.

One of the most difficult therapist tasks in REBT, particularly for novices, is inference chaining, i.e. linking the client's personally significant assumptions about an activating event (A) in order to find the one (known as the critical A) which triggers the client's irrational belief (B) which then, in turn, directly leads to his emotional reaction at C. Inference chaining quickly takes the client to the heart of his presenting problem by a series of 'let's assume ... then what?' questions. Some students, after watching an experienced REBT therapist elicit an inference chain from a member of the group who has volunteered a problem, can conclude how seemingly straightforward the process is - until they try it for themselves:

Student (as therapist): What is anxiety-provoking in your mind about getting to the meeting late?

Student (as client): Well, that other people at the meeting might think badly of me.

Student (as therapist): Let's assume that they do think badly of you. How will you feel then?

Student (as client): Hurt. I couldn't help getting there late.

Student (as therapist): And what else are you hurt about?

Student (as client): Well, it's not fair if they think badly of me as I'm always on time usually. I feel they'll be unhappy with me on this occasion.

Student (as therapist): Feelings are not facts and therefore they are not a sound basis for arriving at conclusions, but I'm sure that they have got to meetings late, so they'll probably be sympathetic to you even if they don't tell you that.

Student (as client): I suppose so.

Student (as therapist): So, just to be clear in your own mind, what are you most anxious about in getting to meetings late?

Student (as client):   That others at the meeting will think badly of me but, as you've said, they've probably done it themselves, so I'm worrying myself for nothing.

Student (as therapist):   Good. Now let's move on to the next step.

In the above extract, the student-as-therapist has made some cardinal errors in her attempts at inference chaining:

1.   She has not pursued far enough the personal implications of the student-as-client's fears of others thinking badly of him if he arrives late.   For example, in what way will they think badly of him?   Will he agree with their negative evaluation of him and then damn himself on the basis of it? The rule of thumb in inference chaining is to burrow into the A and not scratch about on the surface of it.

2.   Instead of sticking with one emotion (anxiety) at a time to explore, the therapist asks a question regarding feelings and receives the reply 'hurt'. Though emotions are usually linked with regard to the client's presenting problems, they are analysed discretely and not in a batch as each one has a separate cognitive structure that needs to be explored.   As the therapist has ascertained the unhealthy negative emotion before she initiates inference chaining, further questions to uncover more emotions will throw her off the 'scent' in tracking down the critical A.

3.   REBT therapists encourage their clients to assume temporarily that each inference in the chain is true in order to find out what they are most disturbed about.   Through assuming that the worst has occurred and learning how to cope with it, clients are more likely to have less trouble tackling actual events.   In the above extract, the therapist seeks to soothe the client's worries in the mistaken belief that she is helping him, that is her role after all.   Unfortunately, the balm she has applied is most unlikely to remove his disturbance-producing ideas which will be reactivated the next time he is late for a meeting or finds himself in other situations where he might be thought badly of.   Self-discipline is required of REBTers not to rush to the rescue of their distressed clients prematurely (or meet their own needs) otherwise the critical A will remain elusive.

4.   Disputing in REBT occurs once an irrational belief has been identified and the rationale for its use has been discussed with the client.   Disputing a

client's inferences ('Feelings are not facts....') rather than holding fire until the client's demand about his critical A has been uncovered is likely to put him on the defensive, stop the inference chaining process in its tracks and convey to the client that inferences are central and not peripheral to his emotional problems. As with providing temporary relief in point 3, self-restraint is required in order to introduce disputing at the appropriate place within the treatment sequence.

Avoiding these and other pitfalls in inference chaining, can lead some students to conclude pessimistically: 'I'll never get the hang of this'. Nevertheless, through persistence and practice these students usually acquire the clarity and precision in their use of questions to become competent in this technique as demonstrated in the following extract (the same problem was revisited several months later):

Student (as therapist): What is anxiety-provoking in your mind about getting to the meeting late?

Student (as client): Well, as I said before, other people at the meeting might think badly of me.

Student (as therapist): Let's assume that they do think badly of you. Then what?

Student (as client): I'll feel hurt. I couldn't help getting there late.

Student (as therapist): You've now identified another emotion, hurt, in addition to anxiety. In REBT, we like to work with one emotion at a time so we can gain a thorough understanding of it. Therefore can we stay with your anxiety for a while?

Student (as client): Okay.

Student (as therapist): Let's return to where we left off: what would you be anxious about if they did think badly of you?

Student (as client): Well, just that they would think badly of me.

Student (as therapist): Let's see if we can be clear about the content of this bad thinking. For example, would they see you as a sloppy timekeeper?

Student (as client): Oh! Much worse. They'd treat me with contempt, as if I'm something inferior.

Student (as therapist): Is that what you are most anxious about occurring or is it something we've touched on already?

Student (as client): I certainly wouldn't like being treated that way but that's not it or anything else we've talked about so far. I feel we're getting warm though.

Student (as therapist): Okay, let's push on then. Now let's assume they do treat you with contempt. Then what?

Student (as client, now visibly agitated): I'd be all alone, isolated at work. No one would speak to me.

Student (as therapist): And if no one spoke to you ....?

Student (as client): I couldn't stand it.

Student (as therapist): What's the 'it' you couldn't stand?

Student (as client): What I've always feared about myself.

Student (as therapist): Which is ....?

Student (as client, in a barely audible voice): That I'm a totally unlikeable, rotten individual.

Student (as therapist): So would you say that what you are most anxious about in arriving late at the meeting is that you will be ultimately revealed as, in your words, 'a totally unlikeable, rotten person'?

Student (as client): Yes. That's it, exactly. But what can I do about it?

Student (as therapist): We'll come to that very soon, I assure you.

The student-as-therapist, having located the student-as-client's critical A, is now in a position to help him identify his major demand about this A. She has been able to do this by avoiding her previous inference chaining errors as well as employing additional techniques learnt in the meantime:

1.   She has teased out the personal implications of his presenting anxiety in a sensitive but highly focused way thereby minimising her chances of

stopping short of the critical A, e.g. by clarifying the content of others 'bad thinking' about him she is able to continue the inference chaining process. Another way of keeping on the track of the critical A is to review the chain with the client as in the therapist's enquiry 'Is that what you are most anxious about occurring or is it something we have touched on already'? Such checking reduces the risk of the therapist following her own uncorroborated leads or pushing the inference chaining in a direction that has only one aim: to confirm the therapist's hypothesis about the critical A irrespective of the empirical data.

2. Even though the therapist does not seek to elicit further disturbed emotions, the client says he feels 'hurt' about the way that others purportedly view him. The therapist does not let herself be sidetracked into discussing this newly revealed feeling and, instead, provides the client with a clinical rationale for staying with his anxiety.

3. The therapist refrains from providing dollops of sympathy or false reassurance that others do not think badly of him. She single-mindedly pushes forward the investigation of the A encourages that she is nearing its centre by the heightened affect that the client displays to her questions and the verbal clues he offers, e.g. 'I feel we're getting warm though'. When the client says 'I couldn't stand it', the therapist has the presence of mind to ask an assessment question in order to reveal the nature of the 'it' and thereby finally reach the critical A which the client confirms. Though not shown in the extract, the client in all probability feels depressed at this point. The therapist now has a third emotion to deal with but consecutively, not concurrently (however, if the client's depression became overwhelming this would automatically become the focus of therapeutic attention instead of his anxiety).

4. At no point during the uncovering of the inference chain does the therapist dispute anything the client has said though it would be easy to do so as there are many tempting targets, e.g. 'How do you know they think badly of you?' 'Is it really likely that no one is going to speak to you at work?' The experienced REBT therapist realises that disputing is best deployed to undermine the rigid thinking (absolute musts and shoulds) from which these inferences derive. In this way, emotional relief when it comes is more likely to be longer-lasting (for a fuller account of inference chaining see Dryden, 1995a).

'MIND YOUR LANGUAGE!'

Students, like most other members of society, will usually be habituated to what REBT calls A-C thinking, i.e. other people, things, events, etc will be directly responsible for their emotional reactions, e.g. 'The tutor makes me nervous when he asks me a question'.'Not getting a high grade in my exams makes me depressed'. When they start learning REBT, students are faced with a paradigmatic shift in their understanding of emotional causation - this is known as the B-C connection. This connection establishes the principle of emotional responsibility through restructuring of the above statements, 'I make myself nervous when the tutor asks me a question', 'What am I telling myself in order to become depressed when I don't get high grades in my exams?'. Weaning clients off A-C thinking and introducing them to B-C thinking is an early task for the therapist to undertake but a highly dubious one for the student new to REBT:

Supervisor: You seem very reluctant to employ B-C language.

Student: Well, who in heaven's name goes around saying things like 'I make myself angry when my wallet is stolen'. Of course you're going to be bloody angry!

Supervisor: Like you are now. Who's responsible for that?

Student: You are for talking a load of crap which makes me angry.

Supervisor: There are two separate issues here: first, you perceive my comments as crap; second, you demand that I shouldn't be allowed to talk crap.

Student: That's right.

Supervisor: So you set yourself up as a dictator and deprive me of freedom of speech. Now how would you react if you didn't mind me talking crap but obviously didn't agree with it?

Student: Well, I don't suppose I'd be angry.

Supervisor: So who does make you angry then?

Student: I do I suppose.

Supervisor: Good. I've established a toehold. Now if someone's wallet is stolen and no matter how justifiable, natural, appropriate, or understandable anger would be in that situation, who ultimately chooses the emotional response?

Student: The person who was robbed, I suppose.

Supervisor: It is important not to equate emotional responsibility with blame. So REBTers are not blaming clients for their emotional reactions to adverse events but pointing out to them that there is a choice available to them in how they respond. So the person might choose not to become angry about his wallet being stolen or be only angry for a short period rather than an extended one. This choice is enshrined in the language that REBTers use.

Student: Hence the importance of clients learning the B-C connection if they are to exercise that choice.

Supervisor: Exactly.

Student: This B-C thinking sounds both empowering and frightening.

Supervisor: In what way?

Student: Well, by demonstrating how much control you can actually have over yourself but frightening in the sense, if REBT is right, how much of a false emotional life so many people must lead when they keep on blaming others for their problems rather than looking to themselves.

Supervisor: You could say that REBT offers a radical and powerful kind of emotional education but obviously is not the only one on offer in the counselling arena. Clients are free to disagree with the REBT viewpoint or vote with their feet. If clients do accept our viewpoint and therefore strike out in a new direction, this is not meant to imply any condemnation or criticism of their past behaviour.

Student: I think I'm more intrigued than frightened by REBT so I'm willing to put A-C language on the shelf for a while.

Students frequently stumble over trying to formulate B-C language with their clients and often produce a bewildering variety of offerings, e.g. 'So you make yourself anxious over someone else making you nervous'; 'We can say that your husband makes you angry but he's not responsible for the way that you feel'; 'So can we agree that you largely disturb yourself but you still have a tendency to make others upset?'; 'The point is to show how you determine your emotional reactions to events unless, of course, the events are very serious and then they disturb you if you let them'. In these examples, the students' formulations negate or confuse the principle of emotional responsibility instead of clarifying or reinforcing it. Understanding and accepting REBT's hypothesis of self-created disturbance usually leads to students becoming fluent in B-C language.

Specificity is a hallmark of REBT practice. REBTers endeavour to make every aspect of counselling clear and precise so clients learn a concrete way of understanding and tackling their problems.   Any vagueness, ambiguity or obfuscation in the presentation of REBT will detract from its claim to be a psychoeducational model of emotional problem-solving. For example, students often use stock counselling phrases when trying to identify clients' problems or emotions, e.g. 'So it's something around rejection then', 'The issue is around this feeling of being uncomfortable' and thereby believe they have located the source of the problem or pinpointed the emotion. From the REBT perspective, this is highly unsatisfactory:

Supervisor: Rejection in and of itself does not have to lead to distress. It is the client's appraisal of being rejected that you still need to discover in order to really understand her emotional reaction.

Student: I don't follow: I thought that being rejected was the problem.

Supervisor: That is the general problem. You need to chip away at it until you and the client reach what she believes is the key aspect of it. For example, she might now see herself as worthless, believe that she can never be happy again, think that she couldn't bear living on her own or that life is awful without love. Get the picture?

Student: I do. I'm just dancing around the problem instead of finding its core.

Supervisor: Right. Now with your other client, which unhealthy negative emotion does 'uncomfortable' refer to?

Student: Well .... I suppose .... it's sort of .... a feeling of .... I don't really know.

Supervisor: You see uncomfortable could mean, for example, anxiety, shame, depression, anger or a combination of these emotions. By clearly identifying the emotion we can begin to tease out the cognitive data that lie behind it. By not crystallizing the word 'uncomfortable' into a specific emotion or emotions you just don't know what you are dealing with or where you are going in therapy. The same problem arises when clients say they feel bad or alienated or some other vague term.

Student: So in order to gain the precision you keep on talking about I need to learn how to focus my mind like a laser on the client's problems.

Supervisor: And you can start with remembering that a word like 'around' is not a precise assessment aid - it's far too woolly for REBT's liking. Try 'focus on' and 'be clear about'.

Student: Okay, I'll try to get my head around that.

'HOW LONG DOES ALL THIS DISPUTING GO ON FOR?'

Disputing clients' irrational or self-defeating ideas is a principal activity of REBT therapists. Disputing occurs throughout the course of therapy and therefore is not limited to a particular segment of it or a timescale. This is often surprise number one for the students. The second one is the stamina they will need to develop in order to challenge and change client's long-standing and deeply-held beliefs. And the third surprise is the creative persistence they will need to display to dislodge such beliefs. Students often assume that when they advance towards clients' irrational beliefs with the trident of logic, empiricism and pragmatism the clients will quickly surrender them and rational ideas will automatically pop-up in their place:

Student: Does it logically follow that just because you very much want to be popular therefore you have to be?

Client: Put like that, no.

Student: Do your demands reflect reality? Because if they did you would be very popular and not in therapy.

Client: That's true.

Student: And what's going to happen to you if you hold on to these demands to be popular?

Client: I'll obviously stay miserable.

Student: So there's no evidence to support your irrational beliefs, is there?

Client: I suppose not.

QED. If only it was as simple as that! Sometimes students are so fixated on phrasing correctly the three questions in order to receive the 'right' answer that they pay little attention to the client's actual reply:

Student: Does it logically follow that just because you very much want to be popular therefore you have to be?

Client: Yes, it does follow: I do have to be popular.

Student: Oh, right. Er .... well .... let's move on to the next question then.

REBT disputing does not consist of just three questions but uses logic, empiricism and pragmatism as benchmarks in determining the quality and impact of the therapist's challenges. Hauck (1980) suggests that one's credibility as a therapist is partly due to having a wide range of rational arguments at one's fingertips in order to combat client's irrational ideas.

LISTENING TO TAPES

One of the biggest anxieties that some students experience is having their audiotaped sessions with clients critiqued in a group setting. Some of these anxieties include the following. 1) Believing that their attempts at REBT are abysmal and therefore they will show themselves to be thoroughly incompetent (ego anxiety leading to shame). 2) Believing that they should not have to put up with the uncertainty of when it will be their turn to present a tape and, instead, should be the first to be heard (discomfort anxiety leading to anger). 3) Believing that they should be immediately proficient at REBT but the tapes will reveal the opposite (ego anxiety leading to guilt and/or anger). 4) Attempting to minimise the 'awfulness' of their tape by making a lot of excuses before they present it (ego and discomfort anxiety leading to shame/and or depression). 5) Exempting themselves from presenting a tape because of the many difficulties they experienced that ultimately prevented them from taping a session (anticipatory ego anxiety leading to temporary relief).

By using these various emotional reactions, students can practise the ABC's of REBT upon themselves and thereby elicit their disturbance-inducing or 'hot' cognitions. Producing tapes for supervision is an essential part of REBT trainees' skills development. The quicker they can overcome their disturbance about hearing themselves conducting counselling, the quicker they will be able to use the constructive criticism from supervision to improve their performance as a therapist (see Dryden, 1987).

Teaching REBT can become a dull affair if the trainers deliver it by rote: stale and unimaginative in execution and dispiriting for the students to watch. The challenge for the trainers is to recreate for the students the exciting potential and reality of REBT that they once discovered but now may take for granted. In this way, teaching REBT is usually a vivid learning experience for both the students and trainers.

CHAPTER TEN

HOW WE USED REBT TO OVERCOME OUR EMOTIONAL PROBLEMS

WINDY DRYDEN

When I was about four, I developed a stammer which led to a long and persistent period of teasing by my schoolmates in primary and secondary school. As a result, I began to view myself as a bit of a freak which, not surprisingly, hardly helped me to overcome my speech problem. I was taken (and in some instances dragged) to a variety of speech therapists over the ensuing years who uniformly failed to help me one iota with my stammer. I began to withdraw from talking in public, loathed speaking on the telephone and would literally quake with fear if anybody asked me my surname - which at the time was "Denbin" [2] since I would give a good impression of a machine gun being fired while trying to pronounce it. I did not have a clear idea of the "cause" of my anxiety, believing wrongly that the prospect of stammering was the main determinant rather than the "awfulness" of such a prospect. In my teens, I went to a local elocution teacher who taught me how to speak on the breath and this helped quite a bit, although I was still anxious about speaking in public. It was only when I reached my early twenties that I got my first real concrete help in overcoming my speech anxiety. This came when I saw Michael Bentine on television relating how he overcame his stammering problem. He told himself, "If I stammer, I stammer, too bad", or a similar variant. This seemed eminently sensible to me and I resolved to try this, albeit replacing his "too bad" with my more evocative "fuck it!" I simultaneously came to the conclusion that I had, up to that point, been defining myself as a "stammerer", which of course, was an over-generalisation. I undertook to re-define myself as a person who stammered at times, who spoke fluently at other times and who did a thousand and one other things, too. With these two cognitive techniques I helped myself to a great extent, particularly when I backed them up with a fair measure of in-vivo exposure. I literally forced myself to speak up in various social situations while reminding myself that I could tolerate the discomfort of doing so. All these techniques, I subsequently discovered, are frequently employed in REBT. I had, at that time, not heard of psychotherapy let alone REBT. Using these techniques, I have, to date,

[2] I changed my name from David Denbin to Windy Dryden mainly to avoid feelings of embarrassment concerning my difficulties in pronouncing "Debin". I changed my first name to Windy because it was a nickname given me in my saxophone playing days, and because I liked it. Dryden was the name of our local telephone exchange. I sometimes joke that if I had lived in the next street I would have been called Windy Wordsworth since Wordsworth was the name of their exchange!

nicely stammered (and more frequently spoke fluently) in various countries without anxiety and can now speak for an hour on local radio without much apprehension and free from anxiety. I achieved this largely as a result of my own efforts (with help from my elocution teacher) and enjoyed the fact that I was the major source of my own improvement.

In the mid 1970's, I trained as a counsellor, being schooled mainly in client-centred and psychoanalytic approaches. I entered therapy, at that time, partly because I thought it was a good idea for a trainee counsellor to be in "personal therapy"; but mainly because I was somewhat depressed. I had three relatively brief periods of psychoanalytic therapy with different practitioners. I found these experiences unhelpful in lifting my mood, was given no guidance on how to help myself and found most of the therapists' interventions puzzling, to say the least. One of my therapists slipped in, as it were, some psychodramatic techniques which helped me to "see" that my problem basically involved feelings of inadequacy. These were unfortunately traced back to my childhood which distracted me from solving my mood problem. I decided at the end of my third unsuccessful therapy that enough was enough and that I'd better help myself as best I could. I turned to Ellis & Harper's (1975) book - A New Guide To Rational Living because it stressed the use of self-help methods and because its content reminded me of my own successful efforts at overcoming my speech anxiety. I resolved to stop putting myself down, to accept myself as a fallible human being no matter what, and again pushed myself to do a number of things I wanted to do but was scared of doing because of the perceived threat to my "fragile ego". My depression lifted rather quickly and I began to feel more alive. All this without delving into my "sacred" childhood.

I remembered, at this time, that my clients had, from the beginning of my counselling career, asked for more specific help than I was providing them with through my reflections, clarifications and interpretations. I resolved to get trained in REBT, believing then, as I do now, that it is important to be trained in counselling methods before using them with clients. This I did and I noted that (1) the large majority of my clients liked my new, more active-directive counselling approach, and (2) 1 felt more congruent practising REBT. I seemed to have found my theoretical and practical counselling niche.

Since then, I have continued to use REBT on myself. I have employed its methods to overcome my anxiety about making an important career decision. I decided, as a result, to leave my full-time tenured academic position at Aston University, taking voluntary redundancy. Unfortunately, I overestimated my employability and was unemployed for two years during which time I coped with my new status with disappointment but did not make myself depressed. During this two year period I applied for and was rejected for 54 jobs or new positions. When I told people about the job rejections, they invariably replied "How depressing for you!". This implies that the job rejections were intrinsically depressing. We hope that you can now see that this is an example of A-C thinking. In fact, I was never depressed and often say that while I received 54 job rejections, I experienced zero self-rejections - meaning that I did not once put myself down during this period.

REBT helped me in particular to overcome my anger about being turned down for re-training as a clinical psychologist. On being rejected, I began to believe such self-defeating ideas as "How dare they refuse ME. Who do they think they are? They should accept such a fine fellow and a scholar as myself and one with such good credentials to boot!" Noting that I was angry, I first accepted myself for needlessly angering myself and then disputed my irrational ideas. "Why shouldn't these people have their own (albeit, in my view, misguided) opinions which lead them to reject me?" The answer, in both cases was the same: NO DAMNED REASON. I reminded myself that while I considered them to be wrong, they don't have to be right, and they are obviously right from their perspective. For a period I remained annoyed about their decisions whenever I thought about it - but was never damningly angry.

I have, thus, gained more therapeutic benefit from my own rational emotive behavioral self-help methods than from formal therapy. Consequently I believe that my preferred therapy orientation - REBT - reflects both my decided preference for helping myself in my own life and my view that therapists had better actively and directly aid clients to help themselves in their lives. REBT nicely succeeds, for me, in both respects.

JACK GORDON

I would like to offer you another example of how REBT was used to overcome a personal problem. In the process of doing so, I will use the material to draw out two important lessons which may stand you in good stead when you come to use REBT, either on yourself, or when working on your clients' problems. Consider the problem of anger. First, it is important to recognise that anger can take several forms. Equally important is the recognition of the fact that anger can be used as a cover-up for something else. Take what is perhaps the commonest form of anger - "damning anger". Here you infer that some important goal has been frustrated, and that some person has broken a personal rule of behaviour deemed important in your personal domain. Your anger arises from your demanding that such frustrations of your goals and the transgression of an important rule of social or interpersonal behaviour absolutely should not have happened; and because it did happen, the individual responsible deserves condemnation and punishment for his or her damnable deed.

Another form of anger, which in REBT is known as "angry hurt", arises when you infer that you have been treated "unfairly" and badly by some significant other, such as a spouse or lover. Let's say you have been "let down". You were promised something you had set great store on getting - a trip to Paris, a second honeymoon or something like that, and that lousy so-and-so of a boyfriend cancelled it and went off to a rugby international with his club friends. A typical reaction would be sobbing, shouting, feelings of "hurt". "You are no good for treating me like this. Damn your rugby match! You don't give a fig for my feelings. I never want to see you again!" The irrational belief here? It's quite clear: "I do not deserve to be treated like this, and I must not get what I do not deserve." There is also an element of damning anger in this response, but the main feeling of upset is one of "hurt". A common behavioural response in this situation is physical withdrawal from the person whose action precipitated the anger. If you can convince your clients that there is no guarantee that if they treat others kindly and considerately, others will respond in like measure, and if you can persuade them to give up the irrational idea that they must get what they think they deserve, and not get what they think they don't deserve, they will save themselves much needless unhappiness.

I can best illustrate a third form of anger by relating a personal experience I had a few years ago. This type of anger is called "ego-defensive anger" for reasons which will soon become clear to you. A woman friend with whom I had previously had a close relationship accused me one evening of not being sufficiently concerned about her health after she had undergone an illness. As we stood on the doorstep of her house she disparagingly compared my alleged lack of interest in her wellbeing with the concern expressed by her other friends after her return from hospital. Since I had not been invited round to see her and in fact had not been able to contact her for some time and therefore had no opportunity to find out about her state of health, I felt really "stung" by her, to me, "unfair" accusation of lack of interest. I still cared a great deal for her, although our relationship had changed, and I had helped her in various ways, and this accusation of implied indifference that came "out of the blue" was "the last straw" as it were. I foolishly blew my top, hurled angry words at her, slammed the door of her porch with an almighty bang and stormed off.

A preliminary analysis of this episode led to the conclusion that I had made myself angry when she implied that my behaviour towards her was evidence of a personal inadequacy. The presumed inadequacy was my failure to act towards her as a presumably loving person "should" act. Her implication was, "You say you love me, but you obviously don't!" If I acknowledged that she was right, or even if it was clear to me from her attitude that she thought that she was right, I would then have condemned myself for acting in a way I demanded I must never display. It is, of course, important that one's actions are in line with, or congruent with one's expressed feelings, especially where feelings of love or high regard are concerned. My woman friend appeared to be saying my actions were not in keeping with my expressed feelings. Thus, my anger served as a cover-up for my self-denigration or self-downing. But, why was I downing myself? What was essential about being seen by her at all times to be loving and attentive? What "terrible" thing might happen to me if she did not perceive me as loving and considerate of her feelings?

Shortly after storming off, I began to feel extremely miserable. I realised the "enormity" of what had happened; I had acted in my woman friend's eyes not only as someone who didn't care a damn about her, but had lost my temper as well. I happen to be a person who very rarely feels angry. So here I was breaking another personal rule: losing my temper, and to her - of all people. She had in her past relations with men suffered beatings, both physically and verbally, and now here I was behaving towards her just as badly as some of her previous bigoted, bullying men friends had. The result of all this self-downing was a severe feeling of guilt. "How could I have been so damned stupid! I've blown our relationship for good this time. How could I have done a rotten thing like that - bawling her out when she wasn't feeling too well, and her of all people! I'm obviously no better than those other so-called men who mistreated her in the past. Now, she'll tell herself, "You men are all the same!" I really cursed and damned myself until I felt really sick.

This is a good example of how anger can be used to cover up a threat to one's "self-esteem". And the intense feeling of guilt and self-loathing which followed so soon afterwards is also worth noting as a possible concomitant emotional disturbance which you may observe in similar cases (an example of a secondary disturbance). It's certainly advisable to be on the lookout for it, for, as we have pointed out, anger doesn't always appear alone.

First, I realised that anger was not the real problem, or at least, the major problem. True, I had allowed myself to get angry over my friend's accusation that I didn't care as much about her as her other friends apparently did. But why did I anger myself over that? I had done the woman no harm. As it was, I was staggered at her accusation that I didn't care; it was so totally unexpected. And, it was also so unfair! Now, I was getting nearer! But I wasn't quite there yet. Whether or not I had in fact treated my woman friend as inconsiderately as she had implied was not the point; nor was it the fact that I considered her accusation "unfair". The basic question was, "Why is it all important, like a matter of life and death, that I have this woman's constant approval? Is it really true that I can't possibly stand it if she thinks I'm a worm in spite of everything I've done for her? It took a while before I was able to clearly see that I was putting my "self" on the line, that I was making my self-acceptance or my personal worth to myself dependent on whether this woman bestowed her approval on me. I began to get it all together as I reminded myself that my intrinsic worth, or worth to myself, is something that cannot be affected by other people's judgements or standards. Some may like me, others may not.

My worth or value to other people, my extrinsic worth, may vary from person to person, depending on their own values and goals. But, my worth to myself is not up for sale. My worth to myself cannot be placed and weighed on some external measuring scale. As my feeling of worthlessness slowly dissipated, I began to vigorously challenge my other irrational ideas. Granted that it would be highly desirable to win back and retain this woman's love and approval, is it true that I absolutely must have it? If I fail to convince her of my feelings, and she rejects me outright, is that the end of the world? Do I really believe I have no future without her? Come now, do I really believe that? And could I never be happy again?

What rational beliefs eventually replaced the irrational beliefs with which I had made myself miserable? I eventually convinced myself that even if I had behaved in her eyes as badly as she implied that I had, that didn't in any way make me a rotten person, but only a person who, in this instance, had acted badly. I had not treated her badly in my eyes, but even if I had agreed with her appraisal, that in no way justified me belittling myself. "Alright, (I told myself), she might have made me a great partner, but do I absolutely have to act at all times in such a way that I dare not risk her disapproval, because if I do, I might lose her? No, I don't have to act at all times correctly and nicely, always looking over my shoulder to make sure she is not frowning at something I've done, or not done. I can treat her considerately like anyone else, but I don't have to bend over backwards just to hope I am pleasing her. If she can't accept me as I am, tough! I can always find someone else more suitable who will accept me as I am."

It was quite a battle. On the intellectual level I was convinced by my own REBT arguments. But at a deeper level I still wasn't sure! Now and again, my irrational "me" would say, "Yes, but suppose you are wrong about her. What if she really does care? Wouldn't it be terrible if you just assumed from her outward behaviour that she doesn't care about you and you went ahead and met someone else, and then discovered you could have won her back after all? She is just inhibited about expressing her real feelings, that's all." Such are the depths of self-deception you can experience when certain irrational ideas hold sway!

In the end, of course, REBT won the day. The other important point I want you to pick up from this account is that intellectual insight alone isn't enough to bring about change. A client may say, as I did in the above example, "yes, I see the truth of what you're saying, BUT..." Whenever, your clients start "Yes, butting", be on the alert to do further work on disputing and to use other techniques if your clients are to make real headway against their engrained irrational beliefs and dysfunctional habits.

As an addendum to my story of how I overcome my own problem, some time later, the same woman tried a little bit of emotional blackmail on me to get me to do her a favour. Her ploy was so patently obvious to me that I had to laugh. It didn't surprise me. I discovered that this woman had a low sense of "self-esteem" (as I, too, had then), and like other people who hold a similar view of themselves, tended to use various manipulative ploys to get people to go along with what she wanted, instead of coming out in the open and assertively ask others for their cooperation. It is easy to be wise after the event, but with hindsight, I now think my friend was trying to "wind me up" or emotionally blackmail me during the "doorstep" episode into doing some further favour for her that she had in mind. It came unstuck because she was quite shocked by my (unexpected) angry reaction. The point, of course, is that even if my diagnosis of her motives were true, her crooked motives were her problem, not mine. The point to remember is that you are responsible for the way the wheels go round in your head. If other people exhibit this or that symptom, that fact may be interesting and even useful in other ways, depending upon the nature of your interaction with them. But your emotional reaction is always your own responsibility. Regardless of their motives, other people cannot make you emotionally disturbed, unless you let them.

MICHAEL NEENAN

I have never been remotely interested in handyman activities such as fixing the car and DIY. I would rather stand in a cold shower for an hour than focus my attention on tackling these things. I am certainly not averse to hard physical work but just the sort that calls for a higher level of manual dexterity. I remember being bored and restless at school in those classes that taught building, woodwork and metalwork. My level of craftsmanship in those classes was pretty abysmal. As I was not prepared to learn any handyman skills as I grew older, I realised I would have to pay or find someone to do the jobs for me. I believed, and still do to a large extent, that it is better to pay for a professional job rather than put up with one's botched attempts. However, at the back of my mind was the idea that a 'real' man was a handyman at heart; this idea was reinforced by watching my brother and brother-in-law who could turn their hands to virtually any DIY problem and make a superb job of it.

I knew I could not spend my whole life avoiding DIY tasks and therefore when I could not find anyone to do them for me or I was too embarrassed to ask, I very reluctantly set about doing them myself. Often, if I did not succeed at the first attempt (e.g. putting up shelves; assembling a piece of furniture) or could not make head or tail of the accompanying instructions, I would throw everything into the dustbin or smash it up in a temper tantrum. I argued that why should I bore myself with these things when I could be doing something much more interesting like reading (one of my ruling passions). My partner stated that when we moved into our first real home I would have to spend more time in the local DIY centre and less time with my head stuck in a book.

At first I did follow her instructions and had some modest success with my home improvement efforts, but I gained no interest, satisfaction or self-encouragement to become a reliable handyman. As I returned to my usual procrastination, frequent rows erupted. My partner liked to point out of the window on a Sunday morning and declare: 'Look all the other men are doing something to their cars or homes [a great exaggeration] but you're just sitting here reading the bloody newspapers!' I would verbally lash out at her because, as I later learned in REBT, she had revealed something about me that I perceived as a weakness (ego defensive anger). At times it did seem that I led an unbalanced life: too much reading and not enough getting my hands dirty.

When I started training in REBT in the late 1980s, I came across a concept called low frustration tolerance (LFT), sometimes humorously termed "I-can't-stand-it-itis". This refers to an individual's perceived inability to endure struggle, discomfort or frustration in his/her life and would therefore suffer grievously if he/she had to actually undergo such travail. So this was what I was afflicted with - it came as a revelation. The fact that I found DIY boring never seemed a plausible explanation for my often deplorable behaviour.

However, with this insight came no immediate benefits because I now had to engage in what Ellis calls 'hard work and practice' in order to raise my level of frustration tolerance. This meant actively seeking DIY chores to do and learning how to accomplish them with some degree of competence (I still paid my brother to carry out the more ambitious tasks such as wallpapering the whole flat). At moments of backsliding I forcefully reminded myself there was absolutely no reason why the looming task must be easy, enjoyable or interesting and therefore 'get on with it!'. Since this revelation, I have been striving to get on with it with varying degrees of success but have not achieved the desired REBT goal of high frustration tolerance. I see myself at a midway point between LFT and HFT: moderate frustration tolerance (MFT).

The greater success has been in ridding myself of the ego disturbance aspects of LFT, i.e. damning myself as weak or inferior because I would not tolerate the struggle involved in becoming a competent DIYer. I no longer feel any shame when someone chides me for my DIY dithering and therefore do not react with anger. I am able to accept myself fully with my DIY deficiencies though I am still critical of my behaviour when I notice I am seeking excuses to put off a particular task.

The excellent concept of LFT has helped me to focus on other problematic areas in my life such as learning to tolerate without disturbance inordinately long meetings, individuals expressing politically correct views, people who want to engage me in extended chit-chat, and anything that seems drawn-out for no discernible purpose. In these situations I was sometimes abrupt (some said abrasive) to the point of rudeness. This change of attitude obviously does not preclude me from expressing my opinions constructively in these same situations and also allows me to feel more relaxed. In conclusion, REBT has helped me as much as it has some of my clients.

We hope that our personal experiences have illuminated your understanding of REBT and that you can now see how you can use REBT both practically with your clients and personally with yourself. Good luck on both counts

BIBLIOGRAPHY

Beutler, L.E.(1983). *Eclectic psychotherapy. A systematic approach.* New York: Pergamon Press.

DiGiuseppe, R., Leaf, R., & Linscott, J. (1993). The therapeutic relationship in rational-emotive therapy: Some preliminary data. *Journal of Rational-Emotive and Cognitive-Behavior Therapy* **11**, 223-233.

Dryden, W. (1984). Rational-emotive therapy. In W. Dryden (Ed.), *Individual therapy in Britain.* London: Harper & Row.

Dryden, W. (1987). *Current issues in rational-emotive therapy.* Beckenham, Kent: Croom Helm.

Dryden, W. (Ed.). (1989). *Howard Young - Rational therapist: Seminal papers in rational-emotive therapy.* Loughton, Essex: Gale Centre Publications.

Dryden, W. (1990). *Rational-emotive counselling in action.* London: Sage.

Dryden, W. (1994a). *Invitation to rational-emotive psychology.* London: Whurr.

Dryden, W. (1994b). *Progress in rational emotive behaviour therapy.* London: Whurr.

Dryden, W. (1994c). *Overcoming guilt.* London: Sheldon Press.

Dryden, W. (1994d). *Ten steps to positive living.* London: Sheldon Press.

Dryden, W. (1995a). *Preparing for client change in rational emotive behaviour therapy.* London: Whurr.

Dryden, W. (1995b). *Facilitating client change in rational emotive behaviour therapy.* London: Whurr.

Dryden, W. and Gordon, J. (1990). *What is rational-emotive therapy?* Loughton, Essex: Gale Centre Publications.

Dryden, W., & Yankura, J. (1993). *Counselling individuals: A rational-emotive handbook.* London: Whurr Publishers.

Ellis, A. (1959). Requisite conditions for basic personality change. *Journal of Consulting Psychology*, **23**, 538-540.

Ellis, A. (1962). *Reason and emotion in psychotherapy.* New York: Lyle Stuart.

Ellis, A. (1976). The biological basis of human irrationality. *Journal of Individual Psychology*, **32**, 145-168.

Ellis, A. (1978). What people can do for themselves to cope with stress. In C.L. Cooper, and R. Payne (Eds.), *Stress at work.* Chichester: Wiley.

Ellis, A. (1979). The practice of rational-emotive therapy. In A. Ellis & J.M. Whiteley (Eds.), *Theoretical and empirical foundations of rational-emotive therapy.* Monterey, CA: Brooks/Cole.

Ellis, A. (1980). Rational-emotive therapy and cognitive behavior therapy: Similarities and differences. *Cognitive Therapy and Research,* **4**, 325-340.

Ellis, A. (1983). Failures in rational-emotive therapy. In E.B. Foa & P.M.G. Emmelkamp (Eds.), *Failures in behavior therapy.* New York: Wiley.

Ellis, A. (1984). The essence of RET - 1984. *Journal of Rational-Emotive Therapy,* **2** (1),19-25.

Ellis, A. (1985). *Overcoming resistance*: Rational-emotive therapy with difficult clients. New York: Springer

Ellis, A. (1988). *Unconditionally accepting yourself and others.* Cassette recording. New York: Institute for Rational-Emotive Therapy.

Ellis, A. (1991). The revised ABCs of rational-emotive therapy. *Journal of Rational-Emotive and Cognitive-Behavior Therapy*, **9** (3), 139-172.

Ellis, A. (1994). *Reason and emotion in psychotherapy.* Revised and updated edition. New York: Birch Lane Press.

Ellis, A., & Dryden, W. (1997). *The practice of rational emotive behavior therapy.* New York: Springer.

Ellis, A., & Harper, R.A. (1975). *A new guide to rational living*. No. Hollywood, CA: Wilshire.

Ellis, A., Sichel, J.L., Yeager, R.J., DiMattia, D.J., & DiGiuseppe, R. (1989). *Rational-emotive couples therapy.* Needham, MA: Allyn and Bacon.

Ellis, A. & Whiteley, J.M. (Eds.). (1979). *Theoretical and empirical foundations of rational-emotive therapy*. Monterey, CA: Brooks/Cole.

Gandy, G.L. (1985). Frequent misperceptions of rational-emotive therapy: An overview for the rehabilitation counselor. *Journal of Applied Rehabilitation Counseling,* **16,** (4), 31-35.

Hauck, P. (1980). *Brief Counseling with RET*. Philadelphia, PA: Westminster Press.

Kelly, G.A. (1955). *The psychology of personal constructs.* New York: Norton.

Knaus, W.J. & Haberstroh, N. (1993). A rational-emotive education programme to help disruptive mentally retarded clients develop self-control. In: W. Dryden & L.K. Hills (Eds.), *Innovations in rational-emotive therapy.* Newbury Park, CA; Sage.

Neenan, M., & Dryden, W. (1996). *Dealing with difficulties in rational emotive behaviour therapy.* London: Whurr.

Persons, J.B., Burns, D.D., & Perloff, J.M. (1988). Predictors of dropout and outcome in cognitive therapy for depression in a private practice setting. *Cognitive Therapy and Research*, **12**, 552-575.

Rogers, C.R. (1957). The necessary and sufficient conditions of therapeutic personality change. *Journal of Consulting Psychology,* **21**, 95-103.

Saltzberg, L. & Elkins, G.R. (1980). An examination of common concerns about rational-emotive therapy. *Professional Psychology*, **11,** 324-330.

Young, H.S. (1979). Is it RET? *Rational Living,* **14** (2), 9-17.

R.E.B.T

RECOMMENDED READING

The following books written or edited by the authors of this book are recommended to those who wish to increase their knowledge of the theory and practice of REBT.

(1) Dryden, W., & Yankura, J. (1993). Counselling individuals. A rational-emotive handbook. London: Whurr Publishers.

This book presents a clear and concise treatment manual for the practice of Rational Emotive Behaviour Therapy with individual clients.

(2) Dryden. W. (Ed.). (1990). The essential Albert Ellis. New York: Springer.

This book contains the most important articles published by Albert Ellis on the theory and practice of Rational Emotive Behaviour Therapy together with commentary by the editor.

(3) Dryden, W., & Gordon, J. (1990). Think your way to happiness. London: Sheldon Press.

This book is designed as a self-help book for clients as a supplement to their therapy and for lay persons interested in applying the principles of REBT to their own emotional difficulties.

(4) Ellis, A., & Dryden, W. (1997). The practice of rational emotive behavior therapy. New York: Springer.

This book shows how REBT can be practised in a variety of treatment modalities including individual therapy, couples and family therapy, group therapy, sex therapy and marathons.

(5) DRYDEN, W. , GORDON , J . NEENAN, N .
(1997) " WHAT IS RATIONAL EMOTIVE
BEHAVIOUR THERAPY"

- Easy to read, concise books - includes
the " finger binding Exercise".

USEFUL NAMES AND ADDRESSES

(1) Albert Ellis Institute for Rational Emotive Behavior Therapy
45 East 65th Street, New York, New York 10021, U.S.A.

A comprehensive selection of books, tapes and videos and other materials on REBT can be purchased from the Institute which also conducts training courses for those wishing to train in REBT in the U.S.A

(2) Association of Rational Emotive Behaviour Therapists
c/o The Secretary (AREBT)
1 Jenkinson Close
Newcastle Under Lyme
Staffordshire ST5 2JP
Tel: 01782 631361

The Association has a list of REBT therapists in the United Kingdom. Please enclose a stamped addressed envelope.

(3) Windy Dryden, Ph.D., is a Fellow of the Albert Ellis Institute in New York and an accredited supervisor for training in REBT. He has authored or edited over 100 books and numerous journal articles and book chapters on REBT, cognitive behaviour therapy and general psychotherapy. Windy Dryden is Professor of Counselling at Goldsmiths College, University of London. He is a Chartered Psychologist and a Fellow of the British Psychological Society and of the British Association for Counselling. He is also in private practice as a REBT therapist, and can be contacted at 14A Winchester Avenue, London NW6 7TU. Tel: 0171 328 9687.

(4) Jack Gordon, BA. (Hons), is a lifetime student of REBT, has co-authored seven books with Professor Dryden on Rational Emotive Behaviour Therapy. He currently lives in Silloth.

(5) Michael Neenan is co-chair of the Association of Rational Emotive Behaviour Therapists and a UKCP registered cognitive-behavioural therapist. He has co-authored several books and a number of articles and book chapters on REBT.